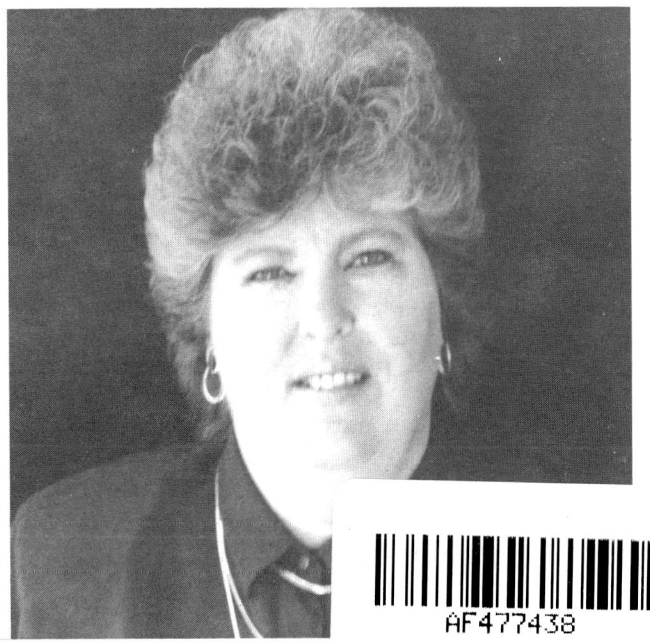

MY HISTORY

Time to write a book? What a joke! I didn't even have time to read one. But, that was years ago when my days were incredibly hectic. Now, my daughter Krista is 25 and my son Doug is 27 and both are on their own. It's been l4 years since I was a Pre-school teacher and 11 years since I took my first tole painting lesson. Since my husband Steve, is a firefighter, I have time now to paint, teach classes and to even write books.

I hope you can find "time-out" from your busy life to spend a little time for yourself and paint with me.

DEDICATION

We took our first lesson together, we go to shops together, we have gone to conventions together, we go to Chapter meetings together and we constantly talk "painting". She is the one I go to for advice, for ideas and for validation. She is my greatest supporter and advocate and she is such a good friend - - - - - - - - -she's also my sister-in-law, Jane McPherson.

As always, a big "Thanks" goes to my family for their constant understanding & support while I do what I love to do. You guys are wonderful.

KATHY McPHERSON
27 Brookdale Dr.
Redlands, CA 92373
909-792-7596

SOURCES FOR PAINTING SURFACES

Most of the wood pieces -
ROLAND NIMMO
9198 Bonita Dr.
Cherry Valley, CA. 92223
909-845-6527

Pumpkin Plate -
BILL GORDON
CUSTOM WOOD PRODUCTS
2816 Newsom Circle
Wichita Falls, TX. 76308
817-692-0950

Ceramic Pieces -
MAGI'S PUTTERY
444 N. H. St.
San Bernardino, CA. 92410
909-888-2701

Bowl with handle -
WESTON BOWL MILL
Main St.
Weston, Vermont 05161
802-824-6219 or fax
802-824-4215

Half Bowl -
PAUL LOFTNESS
Route 1
Gibbon, MN. 55335
507-834-6948

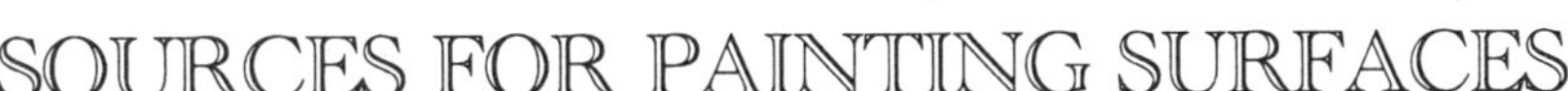

SUPPLIES AND INSTRUCTIONS PROCEDURES

Throughout the book, in this section, I'll list things other than the normal painting supplies that you will need to complete the piece as I have done it. Also, any brush that may do a particular task will be listed here. Below are the brushes that I used to paint the pieces in this book.

Acrylic Brushes:
Langnickle Royal Sable -
Series 5180S Shader Sizes: 2 - 10
Series Kolinsky Wash Sizes: 1/2" - 3/4"
Series Spotter Sizes: 10 - 3/0

Oil Brushes:
Langnickle Royal Sable -
Series 5015 Short Bright Sizes: 1 - 8
Series 5005 Short Round Sizes: 1 - 6
Red Sable -
Series 600 Spotter Sizes: 10 - 1
Series 5533TS Filbert Size: 4
Royal Natural Hair -
Series 9314 China Mop Size: Small - Large
Series 999 Mini Mops Size: Small

EXTENDER

Many times throughout the book, you will see extender listed in the supply section. I use **Deco Americana Brush 'n Blend Extender**. When there isn't a specific use listed, the extender is used to accomplish soft highlighting & shading. Simply, apply to the area with a flat brush (don't puddle it, just cover the area with a dull shine). Paint the area and then mop gently to blend the values. After painting, be sure the area is totally dry before applying another layer of extender and paint as it will lift the paint underneath.

PALETTE

In most cases, the oil pieces were based in acrylic paint before the pattern was transferred.

First listed will be the acrylic colors used & then the oil paints next. I always use **Deco Americana Acrylics** and **Winsor & Newton - Winton Oils**. Occasionally, I will use **Shiva Permasol Transparent Oils** The conversion chart will help you convert to the paint of your choice.

PREP
Seal, Fill, Sand and Tack

In this section, I'll explain how to base the piece before the detailed painting begins. If the piece is ceramic or fabric, specific instructions will be given. Instructions for preparing each individual wood piece will not be given.   All wood pieces are prepared in the same manner:

I always use **McCloskey's Stain Controller & Wood Sealer - Clear 2931** to seal my wood pieces. It lifts the grain of the wood so that you can sand it smooth. It won't lift again, even with watered down washes.

Next, fill any holes or dents with a good wood filler. I use **J.W. etc. Wood Filler**, but any brand will do. After the filler has dried, you are ready to sand. Sanding is an important step to a professionally finished piece. Use a fine grade sandpaper. I believe that an electric hand sander is the better way to sand and the little **Ryobi** sander is great for getting into tight corners. But, if you don't have a sander and you are sanding by hand, be sure to sand completely. Always try to sand with the grain of the wood. I like to close my eyes and feel for the bumps. You'll be suprised at how much better you can feel in the dark.

Basing

The proper basing techniques are key to making your piece look its best. It's better to brush on several thinner coats of acrylic paint than to apply a couple of thick, uneven coats with alot of ridges. Be sure the coverage is opaque, unless a wash is requested. It is helpful to lightly sand between coats to keep from getting any impurities in the paint or from forming a buildup.   If you have a flat painting surface & you are painting in oils, it's nice to have an eggshell finish for the oil paint to adhere to. You can achieve this effect by using a small sponge roller (you can purchase them at craft stores & home improvement stores). Roll the paint over the surface until you feel the roller begin to drag or pull a bit. This will also eliminate any bubbles. You'll have a great surface to apply oil paint to.

Tracing

There are several kinds of tracing products & all are fine. The important thing to remember is that the tracing should be just dark enough for you to see it. Don't trace too dark or so hard that you indent the wood. I've seen many pieces ruined because of unsightly graphite lines. Oil paint is very transparent & lines are difficult to cover. Remember that the pattern is there to help you place things, but you don't need to trace every line. Try not to use the pattern as a crutch. Be creative. Change things to fit your own needs. Eliminate things you don't like. Add things from another pattern.

PAINTING TERMS continued

"STIPPLE" - Use an old brush, flat or round, depending on the area to be covered. Pounce the brush straight up and down lightly. It can be as thick or thin as you desire.

"SPLATTER" or "SPATTER" - Thin the paint to an ink consistency. Load a large flat brush with paint. Use a second brush to hit the brush against. Gently tap the brush over a piece of paper to determine the size of splatters you want. When you have determined this, tap gently over the piece (you may want to cover an area that you don't want splattered with a piece of paper, first). Some painters use a fan brush for this technique. Others like to use an old toothbrush.

"SLIP-SLAP" - Fully load a flat brush with paint. Apply pressure as you stroke the brush in one direction, lift the brush & stroke in the opposite direction. Keep the strokes short and choppy as if you are making little X's. You can completely cover an area or just do a small spot.

"WASH" - Fully load a round brush with paint that has been thinned with water to a consistency equal to tea.To keep from forming lines, work quickly to cover an entire area at one time. To make the area a value darker, just apply another coat.

"GLAZING" - It is a transparent layer of color over another color. To glaze in Acrylics - After the area to be glazed has dried, use **Jo Sonja's Clear Glazing Medium** over the area to protect the paint from lifting. Mix the color to be glazed with a small amount of extender and apply over the area. Mop to blend. To glaze in oils - **Permosol** paints are already a transparent paint right from the tube. Or you can mix the color you want to glaze with and a little **Winsor & Newton Blending & Glazing Medium** to get a transparent glaze.

"OPAQUE COVERAGE" - This means total coverage or no background color showing through. It usually takes 2 or more coats to get a nice opaque coverage.

"ACCENT" - The accent is an area on an item that receives a complimentary color or a reflecting color from an ajoining item. It could be a warm color on a cool colored plum, for example. These can be applied by "glazing".

"VALUE" This means the lightness or darkness of a color. I have used 6 values at most and sometimes less for the oil pieces in this book. Refer to Value Scale of each piece.

"CAST SHADOW" - When light shines on an object, that object obscures the light from passing to the other side. Instead, a shadow is cast on objects in its range or across a flat surface. This is a cast shadow. It should always be painted with 3 values.

"CENTER OF INTEREST" - Light directed on items will be strongest in the middle and will be less intense as it radiates outward. The area that receives the greatest amount of light, whether it be on one object or on several, will be the "center of interest". It should also have the sharpest detail and the most contrasts of color.

"TROMPE L'OEIL" - It is an item that has been painted to look so real that you must look at it very closely to know if it is real or painted. The item is always actual size and painted with a lot of detail. Shadows are important to further "fool the eye".

"BASE" of something - When I refer to the base of something I mean the bottom section or the largest part that comes from the stem, or in the case of a petal - I'm referring to the part that is attached to the center of the flower.

"TAPE" - I only use **Scotch Magic Tape**. It is transparent and will hold up to water better than any other tape I've seen. Be sure to press the tape down really good so they're won't be any seepage. Base with thinner coats of paint to avoid buildups at the tape edge. Lift back toward the painted tape and away from the painted side to get a crisp edge.

"SCUMBLE" - In this book, it means the same thing as slip-slap.

DETAILED INSTRUCTIONS

I'll always start this section with the LIGHT SOURCE. This will tell you where the light is coming from and where to concentrate the greatest amount of highlight value and deepest shade values.

Next, if it's an acrylic piece, I'll explain in numerical order, the steps to paint the piece. If it's an oil piece, I'll list the value mixes that are needed before you begin to paint (see WHAT IS A VALUE SCALE? for more information).

I believe that it is easier to look at the color photo of the piece and transfer the values to your own piece, rather than try to follow a Color Placement Map. There are so many lines and divisions in them, they begin to become confusing. Therefore, I'm leaving it up to you to use your eyes as your guide.

With both acrylic and oil, I divide the portions of paint into parts, with the greatest part of paint listed first, and lesser portions following. Sometimes you'll see a (•) directly in front of a color name. This tells you that you will need a very small amount of that particular color.

FINISHING -

This section will give you any instructions to complete the piece other than normal finishing techniques. If the procedure is normal, it will tell you to follow regular finishing techniques as listed in this section. My normal finishing technique, whether it be in oils or in acrylic is as follows -

Spray the piece with several coats (5 or 6) of Krylon Matte Spray #1311. Use a piece of black wet sandpaper #600 to wet sand the piece. Apply water to the surface and softly rub the sandpaper in a circular motion. After the last coat of Krylon, I use water and a little Orange Oil Furniture Polish (any brand) to wet sand. This helps keep the shine and it smells good too. Sometimes, after I have sprayed, I'll use a brown paper grocery bag to give the piece a soft shine. Cut off a piece, crumple it up and gently rub over the surface.

PAINTING TERMS
WHAT IS A VALUE SCALE?

Every object has dimension. Dimension in a painting helps the objects to pop out or fade back. It is accomplished by using several values of the objects real color. Light values make an object seem closer, whereas darker values make the object recede. There-fore, to make a ball that is one color appear to be round, the ball must be painted in several values of that color.

You will find that every oil piece in this book has a very limited palette. That's because the colors are made from a few primary and secondary colors and are divided into values. Sample color values found in this book will help you match your mixes to mine.

The value scales will read like this: First, mix the <u>Medium Value</u> (this is the actual color of the object). In a couple of my pieces, I have used a <u>Medium Light Value</u>. It will be one shade lighter than Medium Value and will constitute a very gradual change lighter in color.

Next, <u>Light Value</u> is mixed. It is made by adding White (and in some cases a warmer color which helps the object to come forward) to become a value or shade lighter than the last.

<u>Highlight</u> is mixed next by adding a bit of the Light Value to White. On the object, this will be the area receiving the strongest amount of light and will be closest to the light source. Sometimes, White can be used by itself to really make the object shine.

Now the values are reversed and those values that are darker than the Medium Value are mixed. Dark Value is one value or shade darker than the Medium Value and in some cases, will be a bit cooler in color (because cool colors help to make the object recede).

Last is the <u>Very Dark Value</u>. This value represents areas that are the farthest from the light or are deeply shaded from the light. They are often mixed with pure dark colors, rather than adding the value lighter.

<u>Accent</u> colors are then listed. They are colors chosen from the palette that will add interest to the object and may be reflections of objects that are next to it or near it.

"C" STROKE - Fully load a good flat brush. Set it horizontally on the chisel edge. Slide the brush left, apply pressure & pull down. Release pressure & pull right in a "C" shape, without changing the direction of the brush. This may take a little practice.

"CHISEL EDGE" - A flat brush that stands straight up and rests on the bristles of the brush is on the "chisel edge".

"FLIP-FLOAT" - Apply extender to the area. Sideload a flat brush. Float normally. Immediately, turn the brush over & float on the opposite side without leaving a gap between the floats. Now, mop to blend.

OIL TO ACRYLIC CONVERSION CHART

WINSOR & NEWTON OIL	TO	DECO AMERICANA ACRYLIC
CAD YELLOW PALE		CADMIUM YELLOW
CADMIUM RED HUE		BRILLIANT RED
ALIZARIN CRIMSON		ALIZARIN CRIMSON
COBALT BLUE		ULTRA BLUE DEEP
BURNT UMBER		1/2 RUSSET, 1/2 BITTER- SWEET
RAW SIENNA		MILK CHOCOLATE
BURNT SIENNA		ANTIQUE MAROON
TERRE VERTE GREEN		HAUSER DARK GREEN
NAPLES YELLOW		YELLOW OCHRE

OIL MIXES MEDIUM VALUE	TO	ACRYLIC MIXES
AUTUMN HARVEST PLATE -		
PUMPKIN		Burnt Orange + Cad. Yellow
APPLE		Antique Rose
GREEN MIXES		Antique Gold Deep
PURPLE GRAPES		Cranberry Wine
ACORNS		Mississippi Mud + Dried Basil Green
HEART 'N FLOWERS -		
FLOWERS		Spice Pink
LEAVES		Plantation Pine + White
GANDER OF ROSES -		
ROSES		Antique Rose
LEAVES		Antique Gold Deep
THE COLORS OF FALL -		
GREENS		Hauser Medium Green
REDS		Cadmium Red
ORANGES		Blush
ACORNS		Honey Brown
ACORN CAPS		Oxblood
CHRISTMAS HORNS -		
HORNS		Cadmium Yellow
POINTSETTIA		Tomato Red
LEAVES		Evergreen + White
RIBBON		Neutral Grey
MOTHER'S ZINNIAS -		
EUCALYPTUS		Antique Green + White
ZINNIAS		Pansy Lavender + Raspberry
CYCLAMEN STUDY -		
LEAVES		Plantation Pine
FLOWERS		Royal Fushia
SUMMER BOUNTY -		
PEARS		Olde Gold
APPLES		Antique Rose
PLUMS		Violet Haze
GREEN GRAPES		Antique Gold Deep
PURPLE GRAPES		Orchid + Plum
STRAWBERRIES		Napthol Red
DAISIES		Orchid + -lum
#1 LEAVES		Forest Green
#2 LEAVES		Antique Green
SPRING RAIN -		
ROSE		Spice Pink
PLUM, RIBBON		Violet Haze
STRAWBERRY		Calico Red
PEAR, P.W. PUFFS		Marigold
PUSSY W. STEMS		Burnt Umber + White
LEAVES		Deep Teal + Jade Green

Painting Tip

Want to choose different colors than I have listed for you? Here is a simple way to test your choices before you paint them on your piece. Paint a piece of paper or cardboard with your background color. Then paint stripes of each of your color choices. Step back and see if the colors are comatible (or pleasing to you). When choosing your own color scheme, be sure that each color is repeated somewhere in the piece at least twice, so the colors will flow evenly throughout the painting.

THE NATIONAL SOCIETY OF TOLE & DECORATIVE PAINTERS

I you enjoy decorative art and sharing painting ideas with others, you should join the National Society of Tole and Decorative Painters. A unique and exciting organization of enthusiastic painters. For more information, write to: NSTDP, 393 N. McLean Blvd. Wichita, KS 67203-5968, or call 316-269-9300.

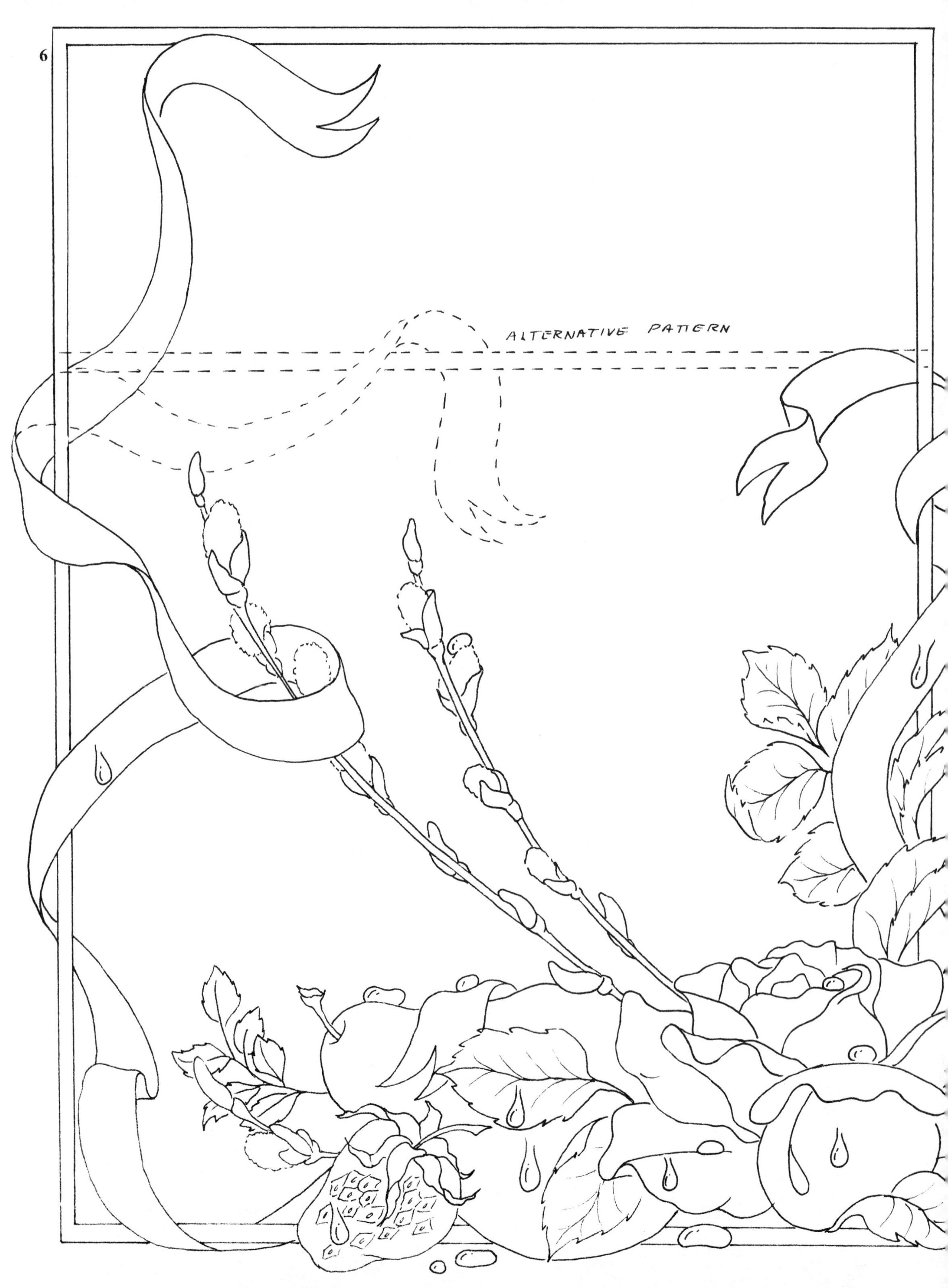
ALTERNATIVE PATTERN

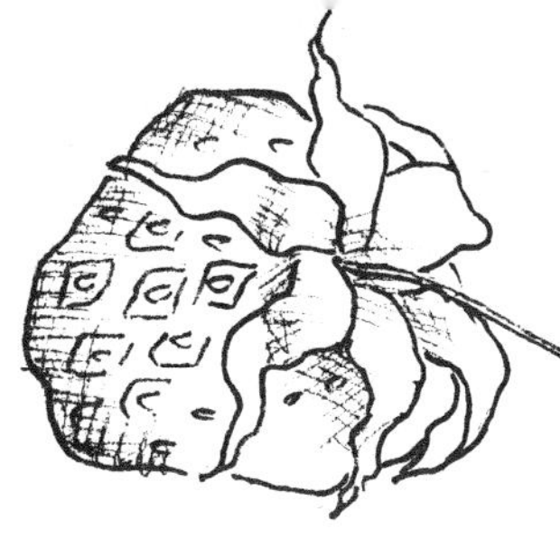

"Spring Rain"

OIL

SUPPLIES   Scotch Magic Tape

PALETTE   **Deco Americana Acrylics**
ICE BLUE   BLACK
Winsor & Newton Oils
TITANIUM WHITE   COBALT BLUE   CADMIUM YELLOW PALE
BURNT UMBER   CADMIUM RED   NAPLES YELLOW
ALIZARIN CRIMSON   BLACK

PREP

1.   Base any wood surface you have chosen with BLUE ICE. Let dry.
2.   Transfer the pattern lightly or adapt this pattern to fit your own paticular piece of wood (by shifting the end of the bow downward on the left side, and reducing the size of the border at the top, you can fit the design on a square area).
3.   Tape consecutively each border line and paint BLACK. Do not paint on areas that have pattern.

DETAILED INSTRUCTIONS - LIGHT SOURCE - Upper left

ROSE

Medium Value -   2 parts WHITE + 1 part CADMIUM RED
Light Value -   1 part Medium Value + 1 part WHITE
Highlight Value -   WHITE + •Light Value
Dark Value -   1 part Medium Value + 1 part ALIZARIN CRIMSON + •CADMIUM YELLOW
Very Dark Value -   1 part ALIZARIN CRIMSON + 1 part BURNT UMBER

Direct most of the darker values to the right side of the rose, keeping the left side in the Medium to Highlight range. The underside of the petals on the left will still receive Very Dark shadows, though.

PLUM AND RIBBON

Medium Value -   1 part COBALT BLUE + 1 part Rose Medium Value
Light Value -   1 part Medium Value + •WHITE
Highlight Value -   WHITE + •Light Value
Dark Value -   1 part COBALT BLUE + 1 part Medium Value + •ALIZARIN CRIMSON
Very Dark Value -   2 parts COBALT BLUE + 1 part ALIZARIN CRIMSON

The ribbon receives the most light in areas that are closest to the light, and usually will cast light wider on one side of the ribbon than the other, resulting in a triangle shape.

STRAWBERRY

Medium Value -   1 part CADMIUM RED + 1 part ALIZARIN CRIMSON + •WHITE
Light Value -   1 part Medium Value + 1 part WHITE
Highlight Value -   WHITE + •Light Value + •CADMIUM YELLOW
Dark Value -   1 part Medium Value + 1 part ALIZARIN CRIMSON + •BURNT UMBER
Very Dark Value -   2 parts Dark·Value + 1 part ALIZARIN CRIMSON + •BLACK

Paint the values of the strawberry as if it were a slick surface. Let dry. Add Very Dark Value diamond shape holes. Place a NAPLES YELLOW seed in the diamonds in highlighted areas, adding a tiny amount of COBALT BLUE to the seeds as they turn away from the light.

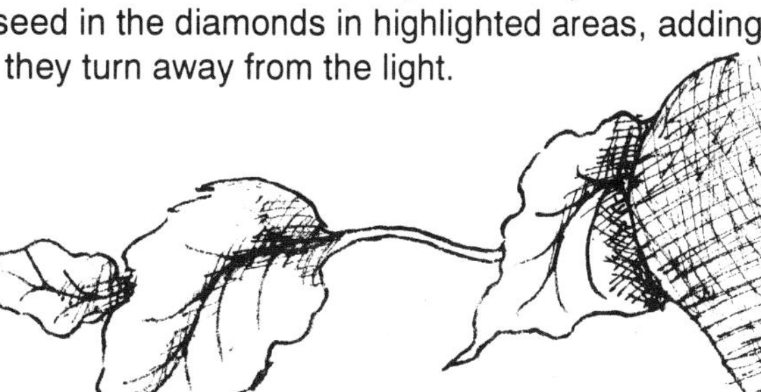

SPRING RAIN continued

PEAR AND PUSSY WILLOW PUFFS

Medium Value -	NAPLES YELLOW
Light Value -	1 part NAPLES YELLOW + 1 part WHITE
Highlight Value -	WHITE + •NAPLES YELLOW
Dark Value -	NAPLES YELLOW + •BURNT UMBER
Very Dark Value -	BURNT UMBER + •NAPLES YELLOW

The pear receives the highest concentration of light near the top.   The Pussy Willow puffs are made by stippling with the appropriate values. The seed shells are Pear Values except - add a stripe of Strawberry Medium Value down the middle and blend into the brown tones.

PUSSY WILLOW STEMS

Medium Value -	2 parts BURNT UMBER + 2 parts WHITE + 1 part CADMIUM RED
Light Value -	Medium Value + WHITE
Highlight Value -	WHITE + •Light Value
Dark Value -	1 part Medium Value + 1 part BURNT UMBER
Very Dark Value -	BURNT UMBER

LEAVES

Medium Value -	1 part COBALT BLUE + 1 part WHITE + 1/2 CADMIUM RED
Light Value -	Medium Value + WHITE
Highlight Value -	WHITE + Light Value
Dark Value -	2 parts Medium Value + 1 part COBALT BLUE
Very Dark Value -	Dark Value + •BURNT UMBER + •COBALT BLUE

The leaves are very soft in color. The two leaves behind the plum and the strawberry leaves are more blue than the rest of the leaves. The vein lines are Dark to Very Dark and are very thin and whispy.

ALL OBJECTS - are accented with the color of the object near it. For example, the pear has accent of red near the strawberry and an accent of purple near the ribbon.

RAINDROPS - SEE "ROSES ON A TABLE - TROMPE L'OEIL FOR INSTRUCTIONS (same as Waterdrops).

FINISHING - This piece should be finished with a Matte finish to keep it looking soft.

ROSES ON A TABLE - TROMPE L'OEIL

ACRYLIC

SUPPLIES -

Stain of your choice (I used Minwax #209 - Natural)	Extender
DecoArt Weathered Wood	Soft Rag (old T-shirt)
Liquid furniture polish (not spray)	Wood Glue
Krylon Matte Spray #1311	Tape and Ruler

PALETTE - _Deco Americana Acrylics_

DARK PINE	HONEY BROWN	BLACK
CHARCOAL GREY	MILK CHOCOLATE	BLACK GREEN
HAUSER DARK GREEN	FRENCH MAUVE	BLACK PLUM
ANTIQUE MAUVE	RED VIOLET	WHITE
DRIED BASIL GREEN - #1 Leaves		
LIGHT AVOCADO - #2 Leaves		
HAUSER MEDIUM GREEN - #3 Leaves		

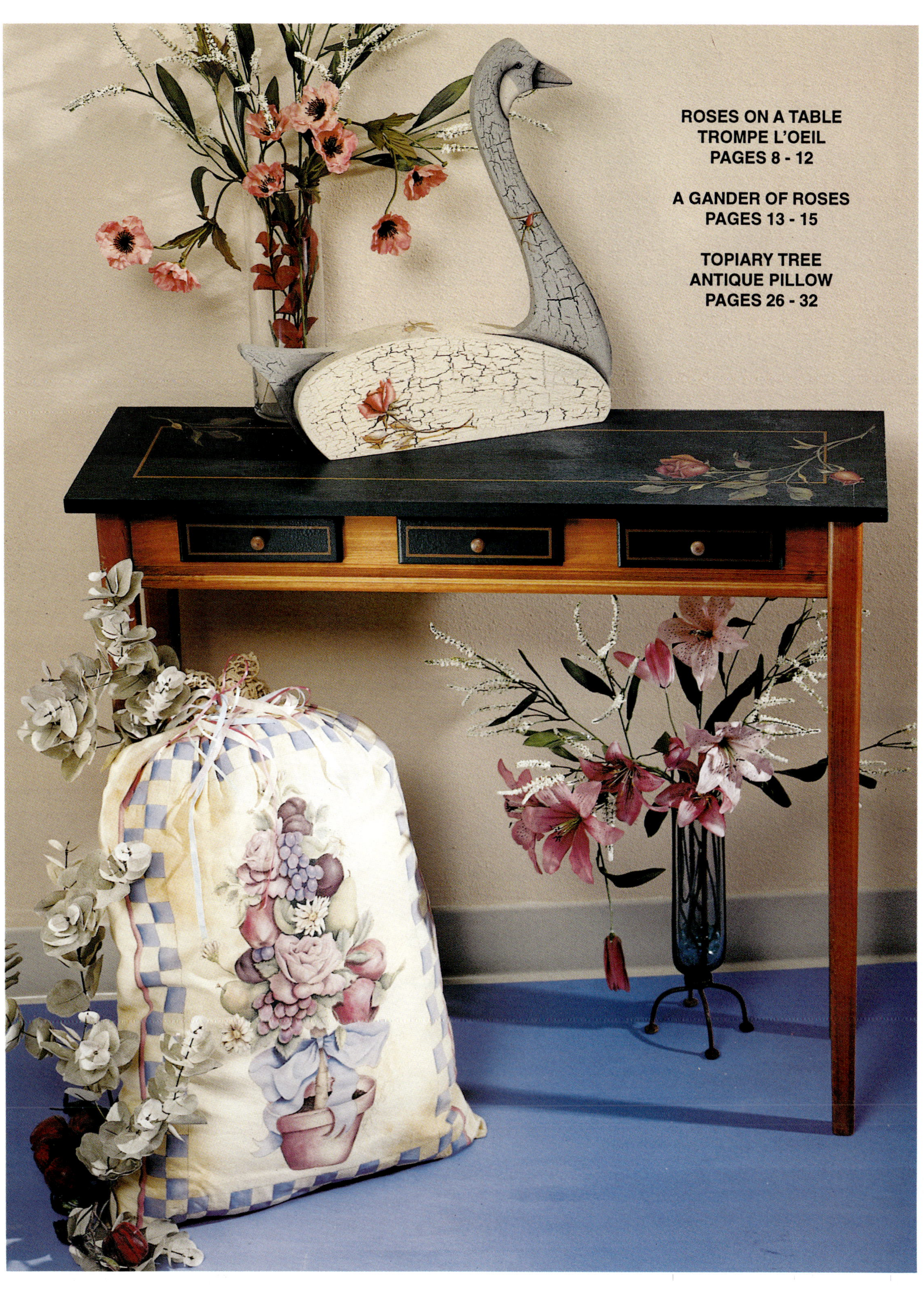
ROSES ON A TABLE
TROMPE L'OEIL
PAGES 8 - 12

A GANDER OF ROSES
PAGES 13 - 15

TOPIARY TREE
ANTIQUE PILLOW
PAGES 26 - 32

HOW TO PAINT A ROSE IN ACRYLIC & OIL

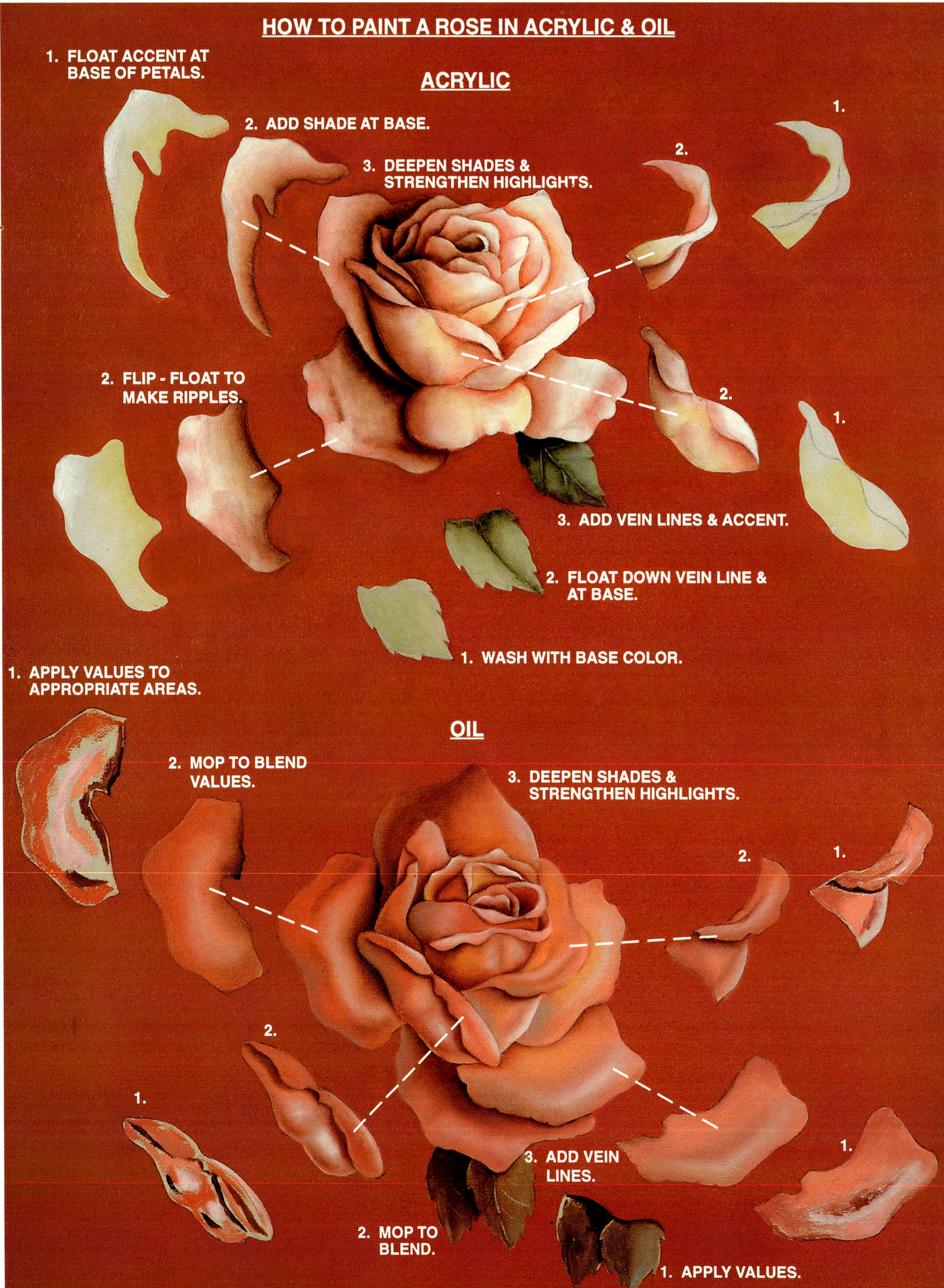

ROSES ON A TABLE - TROMPE L'OEIL continued
PREP

1. Stain the legs and the knobs with your stain choice. Be sure to stain underside of table too.
2. The process for texture on table top, sliding side extensions and drawer fronts is as follows:
   A. Base them with DARK PINE.
   B. Apply a thick even coat of WEATHERED WOOD. Let dry as per bottle instructions.
   C. Apply an even coat of the same base color as in Step A over the Weathered Wood. Let dry overnight.
   D. Now, mix 1/3 BLACK + 2/3 extender (make enough to do all pieces). Using a soft rag and working quickly, rub the mixture over all based areas (avoid going over areas that have dried as it will wipe out what you have done). Work it into all crackles. If it has become too dark, you can wipe it off with a wet paper towel and do that area again.
4. Using a ruler as a guide, measure and mark off 2-3/8" in from the edge of table on all 4 sides. Tape 1/8" in from that line (be very careful when removing tape so that the crackled coat does not pull off). Base MILK CHOCOLATE.
5. Transfer basic lines of pattern onto table top (be aware that some of the leaves are under the border line and some are on top).
6. Base leaves as follows with two coats:
   #1 leaves - DRIED BASIL GREEN
   #2 leaves - LIGHT AVOCADO
   #3 leaves - HAUSER MEDIUM GREEN
   Stems are a continuation of leaf color and blended together into HAUSER MEDIUM GREEN.
7. Base the roses ANTIQUE MAUVE.
8. Transfer the detail lines for the roses and leaves.

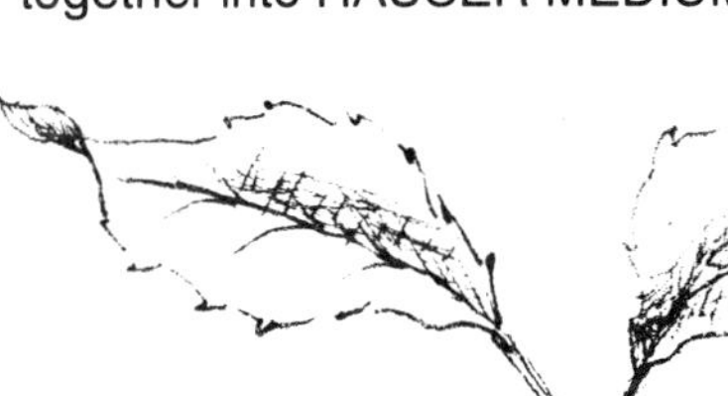

DETAILED INSTUCTIONS - LIGHT SOURCE - above and to front of table

LEAVES AND STEMS

1. Brush mix RED VIOLET + HONEY BROWN. Apply to edges and hole areas of most leaves (no tiny leaves, though).
2. Flip-float CHARCOAL GREY down center of each leaf.
3. Lightly line the veins with DRIED BASIL GREEN + HAUSER MED. GREEN + CHARCOAL GREY.
4. Now, float CHARCOAL GREY between the vein lines. Add HAUSER MED. GREEN in some areas.
5. Highlight each leaf with DRIED BASIL GREEN. Add HONEY BROWN for tint on tiny leaves and highlighted areas of big leaves.

ROSES

1. Seperate the petals by shading between them with BLACK PLUM.
2. Tint the left side of the full rose and both sides of the bud with RED VIOLET.
3. Tint the right side of the big rose and the bud with HONEY BROWN.
4. Deepen the shading with BLACK PLUM.
5. Highlight FRENCH MAUVE + ANTIQUE MAUVE, then just FRENCH MAUVE.

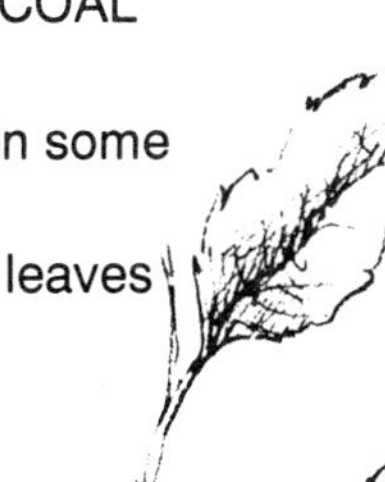

WATER DROPS

1. Line the drop with WHITE. Float WHITE to the inside of the drop line.
2. Use shade color to float at top right of drop. Use WHITE to highlight the bottom left side.
3. Shade the outside of the drop on the bottom left.
4. Float RED VIOLET to upper left of leaf water drop only, ANTIQUE MAUVE to table water drop.
5. Add a sparkle dot to the upper right.

FINISHING

1. Glue the drawers and the knobs on with a good wood glue.
2. Follow regular finishing procedures.

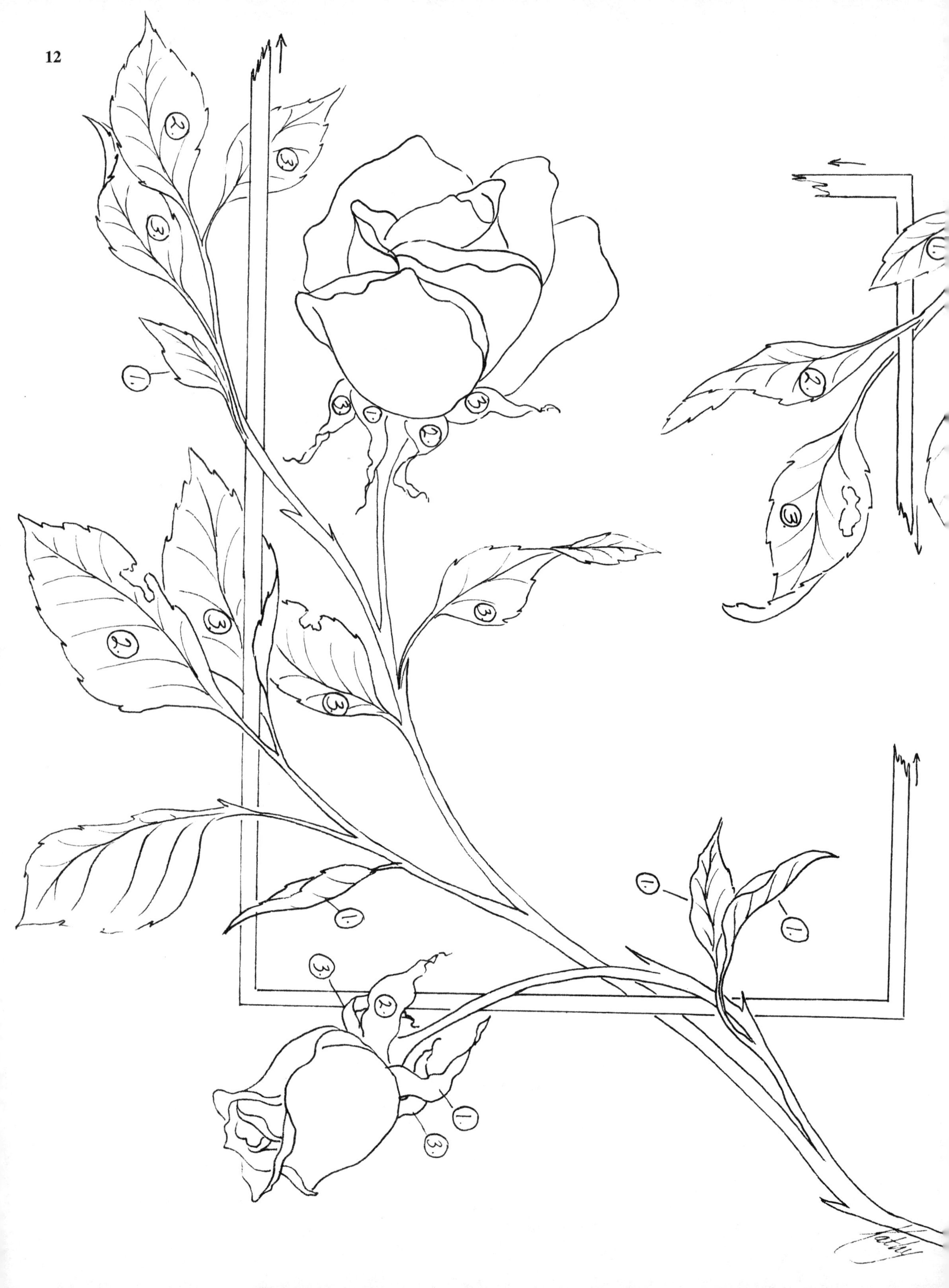

"A Gander Of Roses"
OIL

SUPPLIES -   Deco Art "Weathered Wood"

PALETTE -   <u>Deco Americana Acrylics</u>

SOFT BLACK	TOFFEE	NEUTRAL GREY

<u>Winsor & Newton Oils</u>

TITANIUM WHITE	CADMIUM RED	ALIZARIN CRIMSON
BURNT UMBER	CAD YELLOW PALE	COBALT BLUE
BURNT SIENNA		

PREP -

1. Base the entire goose SOFT BLACK.
2. Apply 1 even coat of WEATHERED WOOD (in one direction only). Let dry 20 - 60 minutes.
3. Base neck & tail sections 1/2 NEUTRAL GREY + 1/2 TOFFEE. Base only body section TOFFEE.
4. Transfer the pattern for the head only.
5. Base the cheek design TOFFEE (back side, too).
6. Transfer the pattern for #1 rose only (because this pattern is so difficult to see against the crackled background, it is my suggestion to transfer the #1 rose, paint it while the pattern is less complicated, then transfer the next and so on. Also, the line placement will be fresher in your mind, (you still my want to keep your pattern close to you & refer to it as you paint).

DETAILED INSTRUCTIONS - LIGHT SOURCE - Upper right

1. Float SOFT BLACK on both sides of base of beak, on both sides down the back of eye to neck, at the front side of the neck all the way down, at the base of neck section and at base of tail section. Later, add Medium Value Rose Mix to the top of beak.
2. Base the pupil SOFT BLACK. Line around the ouside edge, also.
3. Place a TOFFEE "C" Stroke at the front of the pupil with a side loaded flat brush. Place a highlight dot at the bottom of the pupil area. (When you have mixed the Rose Dark Value, place a "C" Stroke at the back side of the pupil).

ROSES -

Apply lighter values to petals on right side of each rose, darker values to left side. Add blue accent to lower left side of some petals. Add yellow accent to base of petals on lighter right side.

Medium Value -	1 part ALIZARIN CRIMSON + 1 part WHITE + 1 part BURNT SIENNA
Light Value -	3 parts WHITE + 2 parts CADMUIM RED + 1 part CADMIUM YELLOW
Highlight Value -	WHITE + •Light Value + •CADMIUM YELLOW
Dark Value -	1 part ALIZARIN CRIMSON + 2 parts Medium Value + 1 part BURNT UMBER.
Very Dark Value -	1 part ALIZARIN CRIMSON + 2 parts BURNT UMBER
Accent #1 -	3 parts WHITE + 1 part COBALT BLUE + •CADMUIM YELLOW
Accent #2 -	3 parts ALIZARIN CRIMSON + 1 part WHITE + •#1 Accent
Accent #3 -	CADMIUM YELLOW PALE + •BURNT UMBER

LEAVES & STEMS -

Apply lighter values to leaves next to #1 Rose. Darken values as you move to left. Stems include light values to right or top, medium values in middle, dark values to bottom or left.

Medium Value -	3 parts BURNT SIENNA + 1 part Rose Accent #1
Light Value -	3 parts WHITE +1 part Medium Value
Highlight Value -	WHITE + •Light Value
Dark Value -	3 parts WHITE + 1 part BURNT UMBER + 1 part Rose Accent #1
Very Dark Value -	BURNT UMBER + •Medium Value
Accent #1 -	Rose Accent #1
Accent #2 -	Rose Medium Value

"A GANDER OF ROSES"

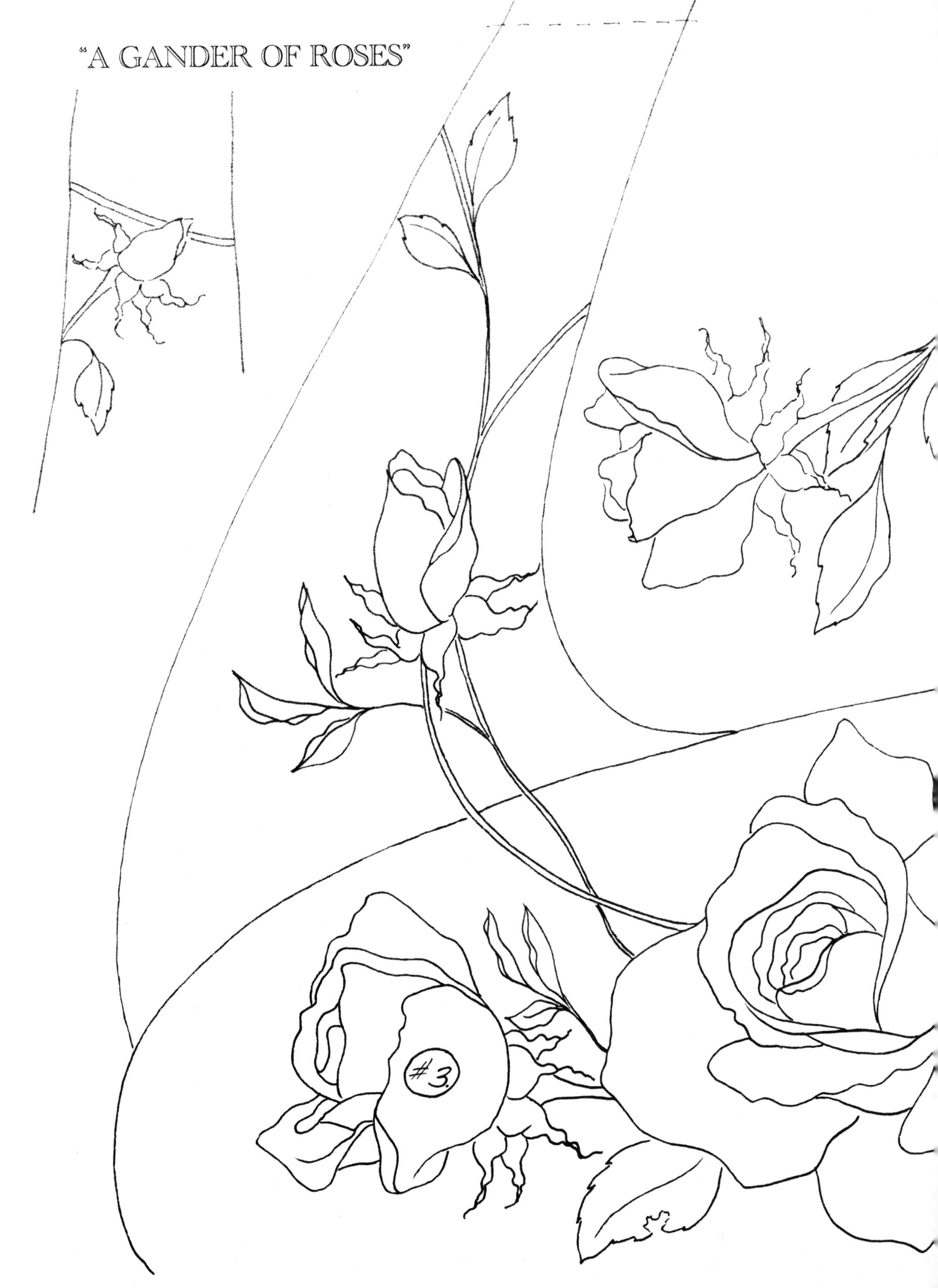

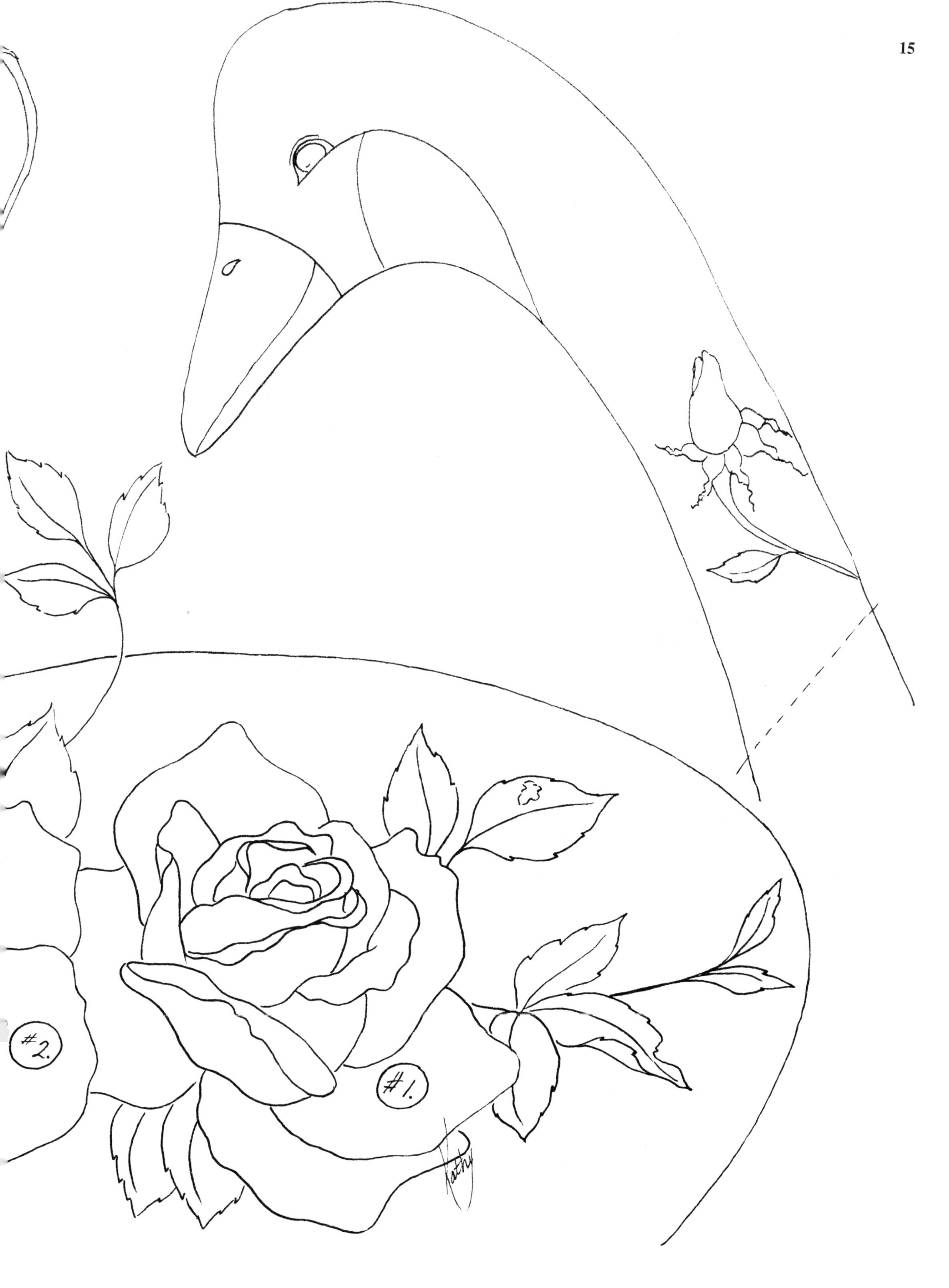
#2.
#1.
Kathy

"MOTHER'S ZINNIAS"

OIL ON CERAMICS

SUPPLIES

Fine Sandpaper   Extender   Krylon Matte Spray #1311

BRUSHES

#4 Filbert   Short Liner

PALETTE - <u>Deco Americana Acrylics</u>

TAUPE	DEEP BURGUNDY	ANTIQUE GREEN
RED IRON OXIDE	ANTIQUE MAROON	TANGERINE
PLUM	HONEY BROWN	NAPTHOL RED
YELLOW OCHRE	BURNT UMBER	

<u>Winsor & Newton Oils</u>

TITANIUM WHITE	BURNT UMBER	CADMIUM RED
ALIZARIN CRIMSON	TERRE VERTE GREEN	COBALT BLUE
CADMIUM YELLOW		

PREP

1. Sand off any imperfections on the ceramic bottom and lid, inside and out.
2. Base the entire piece. Make small piles of these acrylic colors:
   - A.   YELLOW OCHRE
   - B.   2 parts ALIZARIN CRIMSON + 1 part TRUE OCHRE + 1 part PRUSSIAN BLUE.
   - C.   2 parts LAVENDER + 1 part PRUSSIAN BLUE.
   - D.   PRUSSIAN BLUE
3. Apply extender to entire outside of the lid. Apply above mixes to areas of the lid. Do not apply too thick. Mop to soften (keep lighter colors to the middle). Let dry. Repeat on sides.
4. Transfer pattern lightly (just make a circle where the flowers will be, rather than transferring the detailed petals.

DETAILED INSTRUCTIONS - LIGHT SOURCE - Right top

EUCALYPTUS LEAVES

Medium Value -	3 parts TERRE VERTE + 1 part WHITE + BURNT UMBER
Light Value -	1 part Medium Value + 1 part WHITE + •BURNT UMBER
Highlight Value -	WHITE + •Light Value
Dark Value -	3 parts TERRE VERTE + 1 part Medium Value
Very Dark Value -	1 part TERRE VERTE + 1 part BURNT UMBER
Accent -	Dark Zinnia Value

ZINNIA LEAVES AND STEMS

1. Add a tiny bit of COBALT BLUE to each value of above mixes.

ZINNIAS #1, #3 and BUDS

Medium Value -	3 parts WHITE + 1 part COBALT BLUE + 1 part ALIZARIN CRIMSON.
Light Value -	1 part WHITE + 1 part Medium Value
Highlight Value -	WHITE + •Light Value
Dark Value -	3 parts ALIZARIN CRIMSON + 1 part Med. Value + 1 part COBALT BLUE.
Very Dark Value -	1 part COBALT BLUE + 1 part ALIZARIN CRIMSON

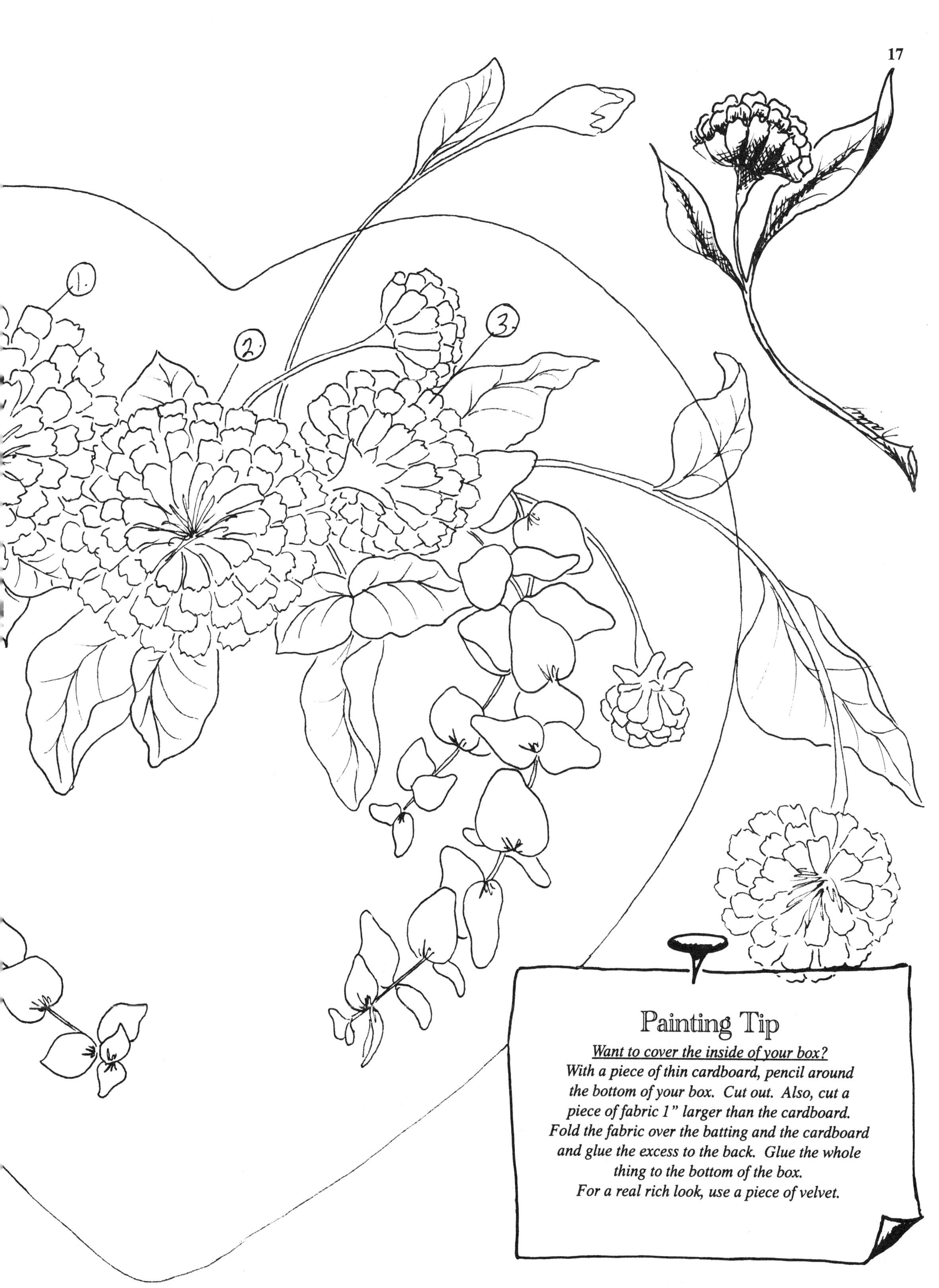

Painting Tip

<u>Want to cover the inside of your box?</u>
*With a piece of thin cardboard, pencil around
the bottom of your box. Cut out. Also, cut a
piece of fabric 1" larger than the cardboard.
Fold the fabric over the batting and the cardboard
and glue the excess to the back. Glue the whole
thing to the bottom of the box.
For a real rich look, use a piece of velvet.*

MOTHER'S ZINNIAS continued

ZINNIAS #1, #3 and BUDS continued
1. Begin by forming the outside row of petals using Dark Value and a filbert brush. When the row is completed, apply a little Medium Value to the petals on the right and a little Very Dark Value to those on the left. The next row is a value lighter (Medium Value) with Light Value to the right and Dark to the left. Continue four rows in this manner (like stacking bricks).
2. Use the darkest value and a short liner to darken and seperate the petals, then blend.
3. Use the same liner, alternate into WHITE, CADMIUM YELLOW and Medium Value to stroke on middle crown petals.

OTHER ZINNIAS
Add a little CADMIUM RED to each value mix above.

FINISHING
Spray with several coats of Krylon Matte. Buff with an old brown paper bag.

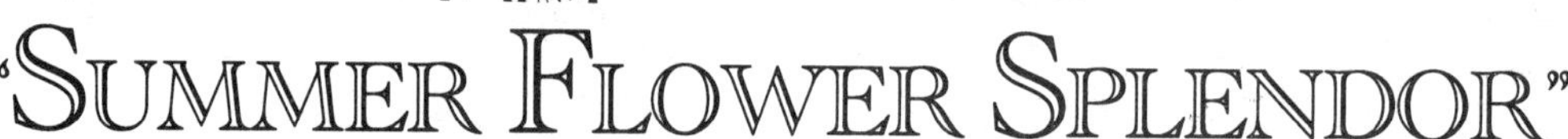

"SUMMER FLOWER SPLENDOR"
ACRYLIC ON FABRIC

SUPPLIES

1 piece of cotton fabric 13 X 17 (preferrably a green stripe)	Sharp Razor Blade
	White Glue
Pencil	Old Scruffy Brush (#8 or similar)
Sharp Scissors	Large Old Scruffy Brush

PALETTE - <u>Deco Americana Acrylics</u>

HAUSER DARK GREEN	PLUM	CADMIUM ORANGE
LT. BUTTERMILK	BLACK PLUM	WINTER BLUE
GREEN MIST	PEACHES & CREAM	ORCHID
WILLIAMSBURG BLUE	FRENCH MAUVE	MARIGOLD
DEEP MIDNIGHT BLUE		

PREP
1. Base the back and sides of the heart with the stripe color in your particular fabric (in my case, I used 1/2 VIRIDIAN GREEN + 1/2 HAUSER DARK GREEN). Use an old scruffy brush to base the areas between the cracks.
2. Set the heart upside-down onto the (wrong) side of the fabric. Draw a line around the heart onto the fabric with a pencil (do not use a felt tip marker as it may bleed on the fabric). Use a sharp pair of scissors to carefully cut around the heart.
3. Apply an even coat of white glue + a little water to the top of the wood heart (be sure to get right to the edges). Carefully, lay the fabric heart onto the wood and work out any wrinkles. Be sure that the stripe lines up straight with the cracks on the wood heart.
4. When dry, use a razor blade to cut the fabric between the cracks (be careful not to unravel the fabric as you cut).
5. Transfer the main pattern lines as usual.
6. Base all flowers LT. BUTTERMILK, all leaves and stems GREEN MIST.
7. Transfer the detailed pattern lines, lightly (do not tranfer the flower centers at this time).

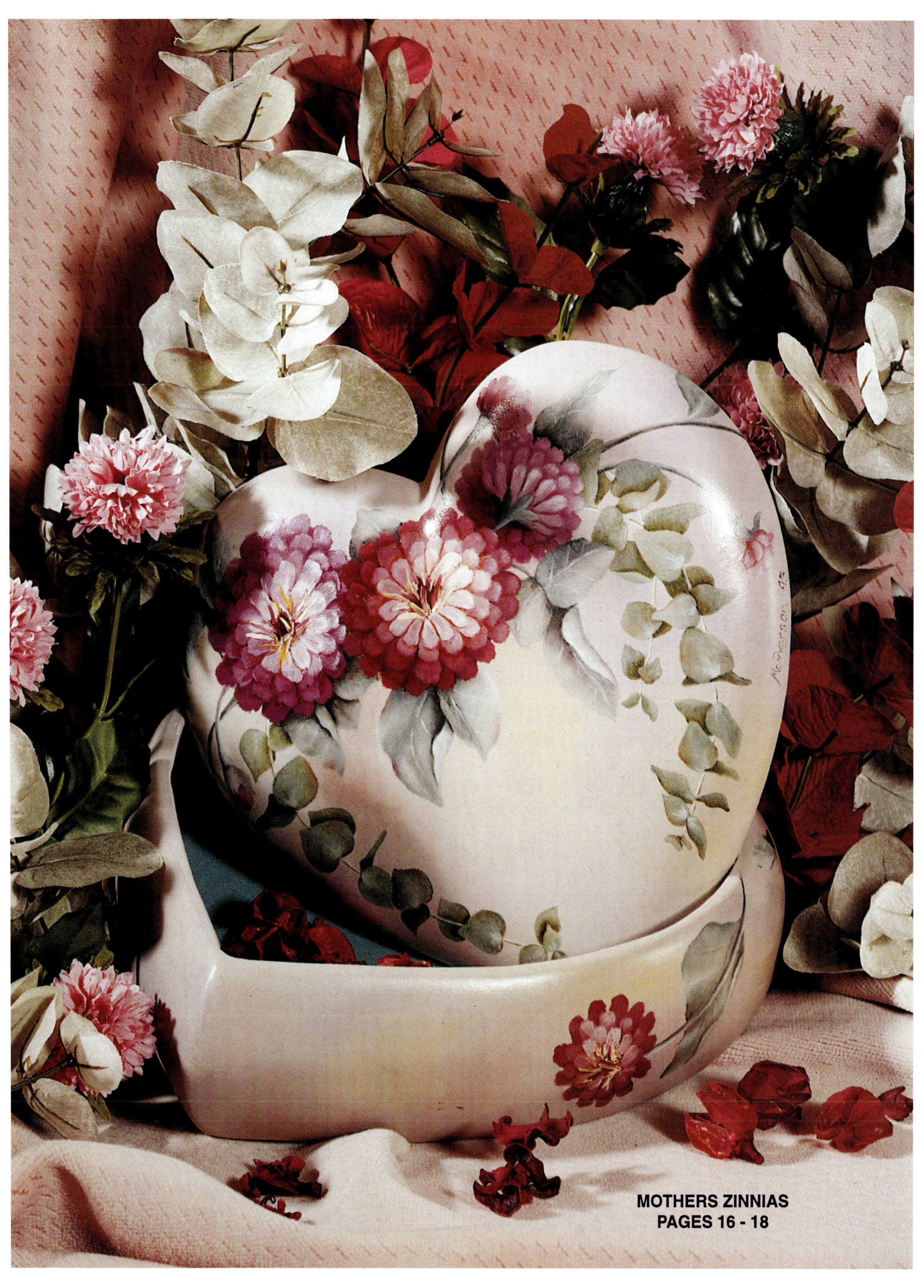

MOTHERS ZINNIAS
PAGES 16 - 18

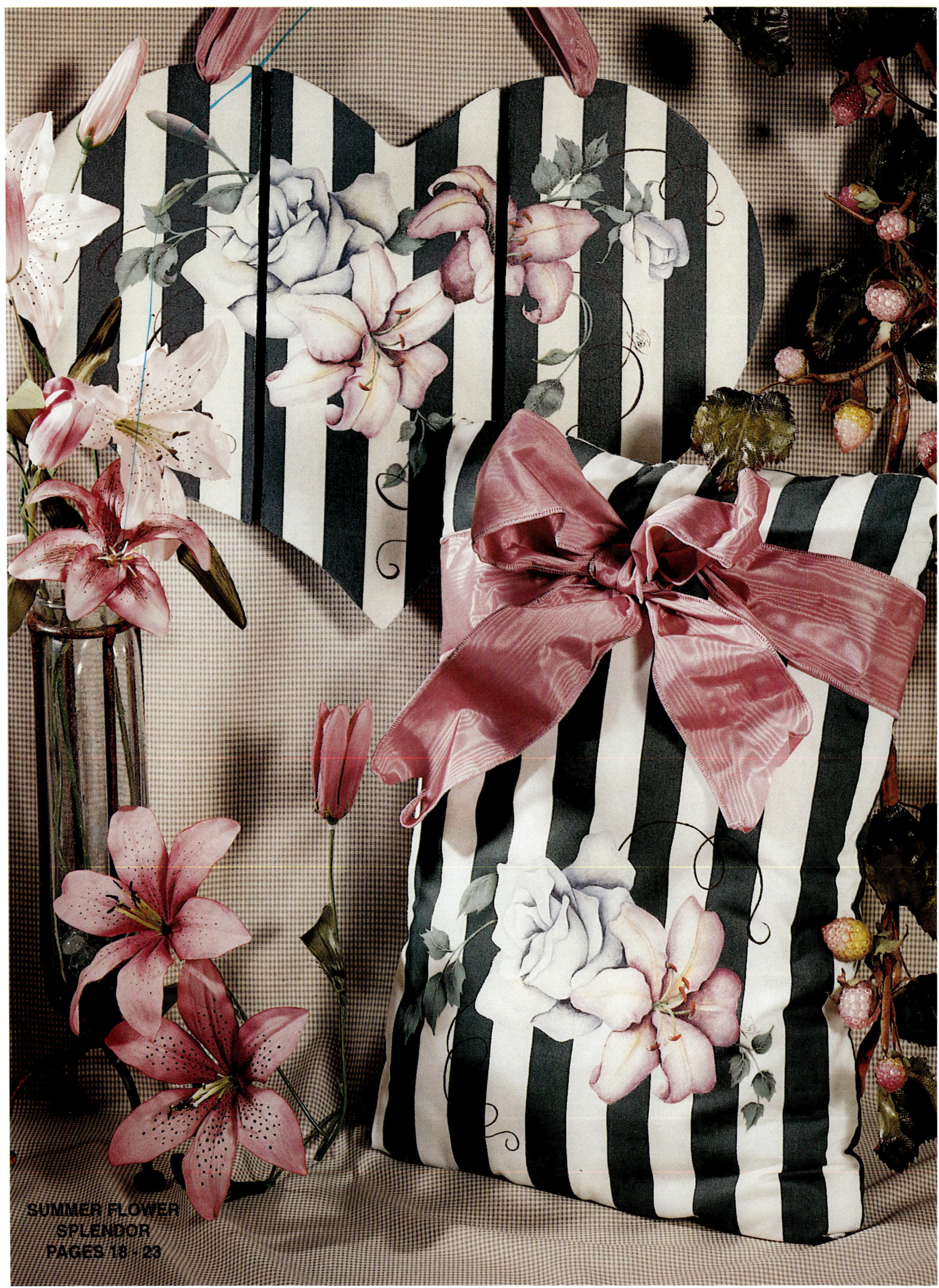

SUMMER FLOWER
SPLENDOR
PAGES 18 - 23

SUMMER FLOWER SPLENDOR continued

DETAILED INSTRUCTIONS - LIGHT SOURCE - Front left side

LILIES

1. Shade at the sides and ends of each petal with FRENCH MAUVE. Add color across the whole petal near the base of each petal (leave areas in highlight unpainted).
2. Add ORCHID in some areas of each leaf.
3. Flip-float PEACHES & CREAM and MARIGOLD down the center of each petal. Remember that the light is coming from the left side, so, add wider floats and darker color to the right side of both flowers. Also, be aware that the flower on the right is behind the one on the left and is darker in color. You can apply a thin wash of PLUM to this flower before you begin shading, but leave a few areas for highlight.
4. Shade at overlaps and in center of each flower with PLUM.
5. Deepen the shade in the center area of each petal with BLACK PLUM. Also, flip-float where there is a curve or a wave in the petals.
6. Accent a few shaded areas with WILLIAMSBURG BLUE.
7. Dip only the tip of one side of flat brush into BLACK PLUM , line down the center of each petal.
8. Transfer the pattern for the centers of the flowers. Line the centers with GREEN MIST + MARIGOLD. Shade with HAUSER DARK GREEN.
9. The tops of the flower centers are CADMIUM ORANGE, shaded BLACK PLUM.
10. The lily buds are FRENCH MAUVE at top, HAUSER DK GREEN at bottom. Streak with same.

ROSES

1. Shade at the sides and ends of the petals on the left side and almost all the petal on the right side with WINTER BLUE.
2. Add WILLIAMSBURG BLUE to deepen the shade areas.
3. The deepest areas are shaded with DEEP MIDNIGHT BLUE (keep mostly on the right side).
4. Accent some petals with MARIGOLD and some areas with FRENCH MAUVE.

LEAVES

1. Shade each leaf down the center and at the base with HAUSER DARK GREEN. Also, flip-float on rose bud leaves.
2. Accent most leaves by adding PLUM to the edges.
3. The vein lines are GREEN MIST + LT. BUTTERMILK.
4. Tendrils are thinned BLACK PLUM (don't thin too much or it will run on the fabric).

FINISHING

1. Follow regular finishing procedures.
2. Run ribbon of your choice through the holes and tie.

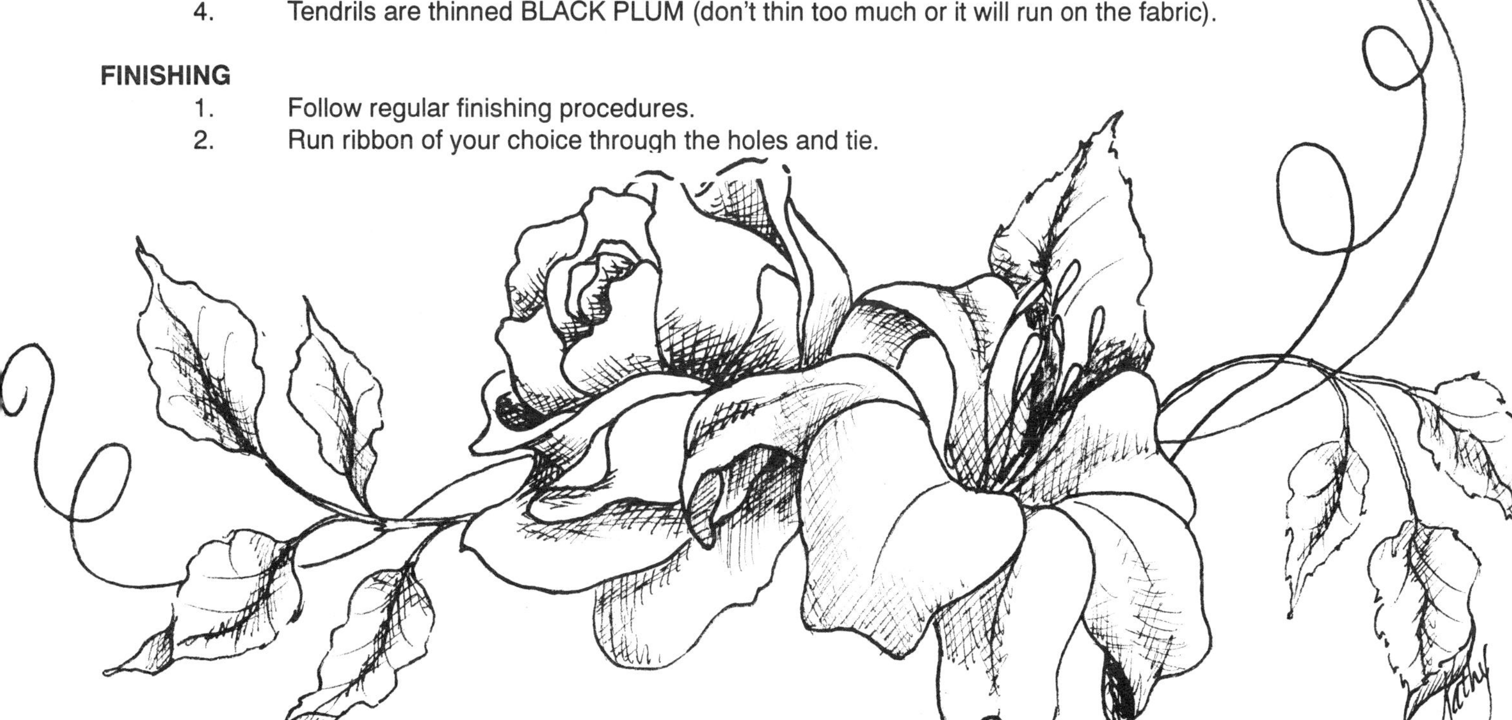

SUMMER FLOWER SPLENDOR

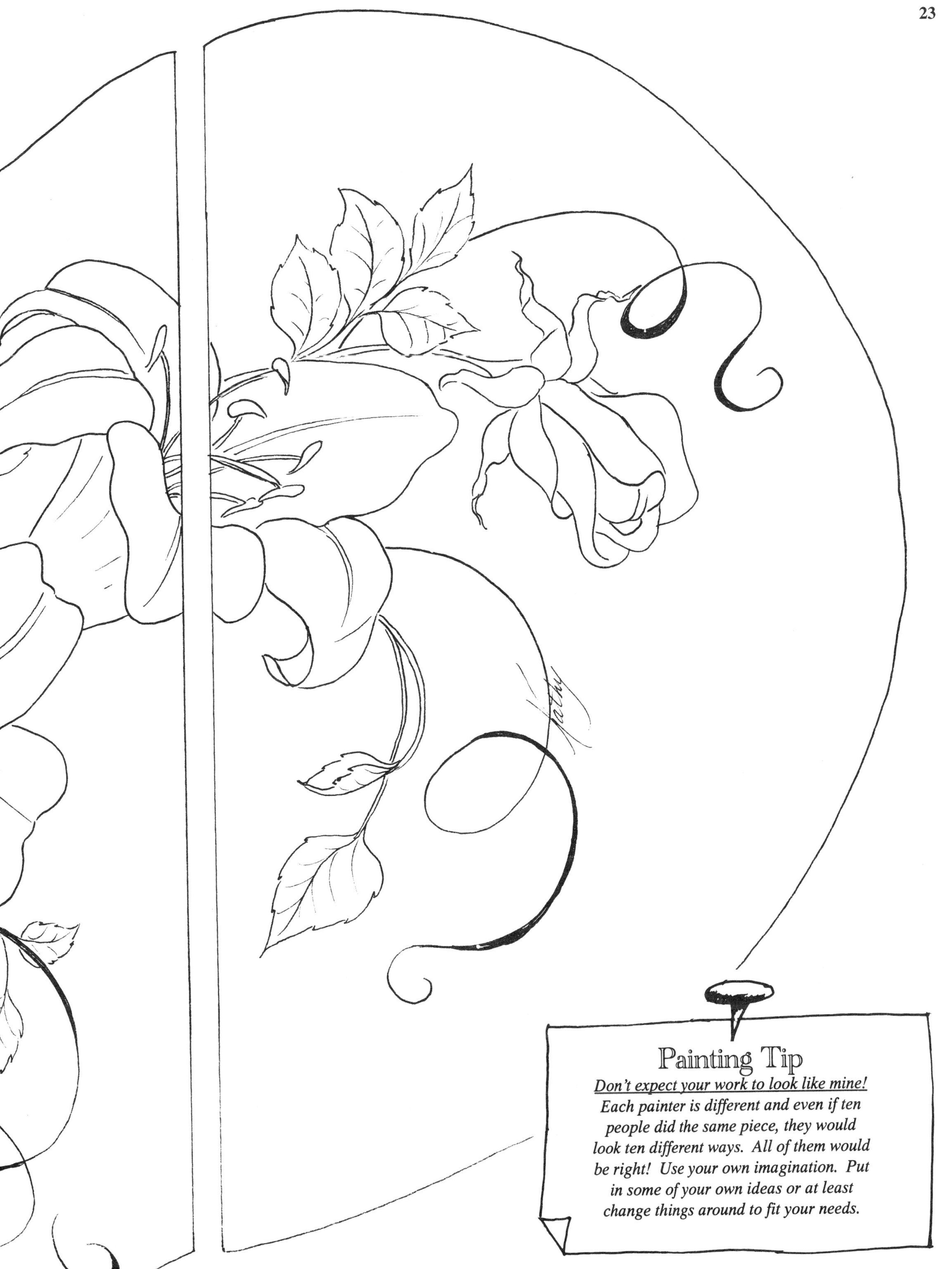

Painting Tip

<u>*Don't expect your work to look like mine!*</u>
*Each painter is different and even if ten
people did the same piece, they would
look ten different ways. All of them would
be right! Use your own imagination. Put
in some of your own ideas or at least
change things around to fit your needs.*

"Heart 'n Flowers"

Oil

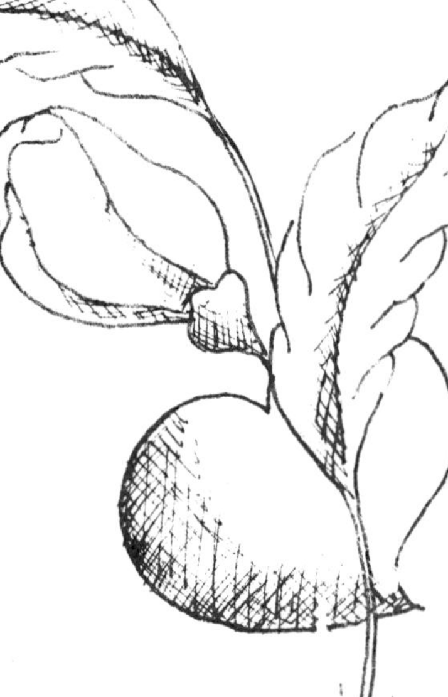

SUPPLIES -

Sea Sponge (with large holes)   Blending & Glazing Medium

PALETTE - **Deco Americana Acrylics**   **DecoArt Dazzling Metalics**
LT. BUTTERMILK   EMPEROR'S GOLD
SHALE GREEN
Winsor & Newton Oils
TITANIUM WHITE   CADMIUM YELLOW PALE
ALIZARIN CRIMSON   COBALT BLUE
BURNT UMBER   CADMIUM RED HUE

PREP

Do not do anything with the dowel that holds lid to base at this time.

HEART BOX LID

1. Transfer pattern for border design only (attn: be sure to align pattern with inside wall of bottom section of box - SEE PATTERN).
2. Base *outside* border line and SHALE GREEN (try to keep from making a buildup of paint at lined edge). Also base sides and back of lid.
3. Base *inside* border line LT. BUTTERMILK (again, prevent a buildup of paint on edge where these two colors meet).
4. Transfer basic pattern LIGHTLY.
5. Base petals LT. BUTTERMILK that occupy the space in green border area. Base twice.
6. Transfer the detail lines of petals and leaves (they must be transfered LIGHTLY).

BOX SIDES

1. Base sides and bottom of box SHALE GREEN.
2. Sponge over SHALE GREEN with EMPEROR'S GOLD.

DETAILED INSTRUCTIONS - LIGHT SOURCE - Left front

FLOWERS

Medium Value -	2 parts WHITE + 1 part ALIZARIN CRIMSON + •CAD. YELLOW
Light Value -	1 part WHITE + 1 part Medium Value
Highlight Value -	WHITE + •Light Value
Dark Value -	2 parts Medium Value + 1 part ALIZ. CRIMSON + 1 part BURNT UMBER
Very Dark Value -	2 parts ALIZARIN CRIMSON + 1 part BURNT UMBER
Accent #1 -	CADMIUM YELLOW + •CAD. RED + WHITE
Accent #2 -	Leaves Medium Value

FLOWER CENTER

Cap -	Very Dark Leaves + •CAD. YELLOW
Circles -	#1 Accent, line BURNT UMBER

LEAVES

Medium Value -	1 part COBALT BLUE + 1 part CAD YELLOW + 1 part WHITE
Light Value -	2 parts WHITE + 1 part Medium Value
Highlight Value -	WHITE + •Light Value
Dark Value -	1 part Medium Value + 1 part COBALT BLUE + •CADMIUM YELLOW
Very Dark Value -	1 part COBALT BLUE + 1 part CAD. YELLOW + 1 part BURNT UMBER
Accent #1 -	Flower Dark Value

FINISHING

1. Glue dowel to the lid ONLY. Insert dowel into hole on the bottom piece.
2. Follow regular finishing procedures.

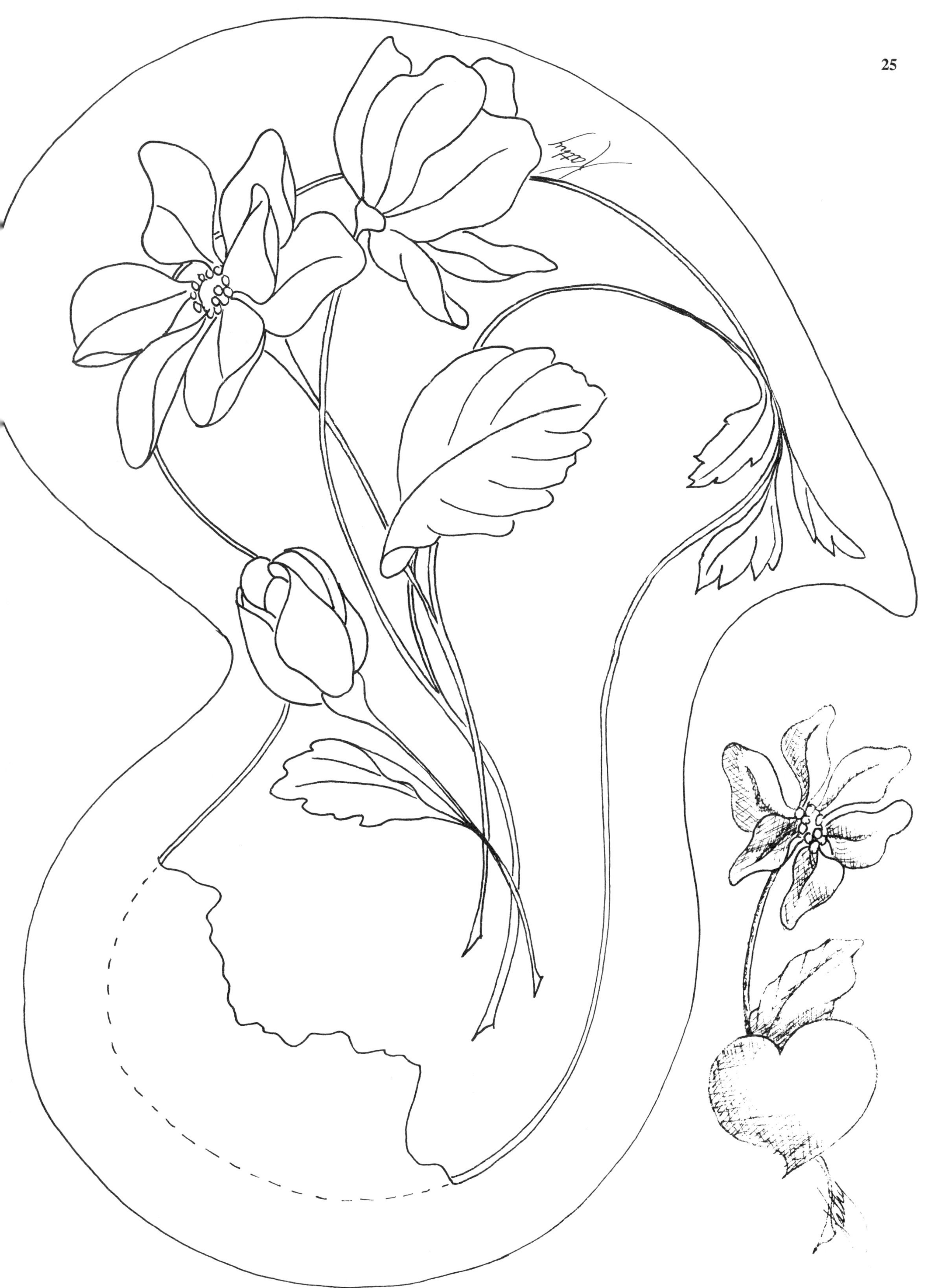

TOPIARY TREE - ANTIQUE PILLOW

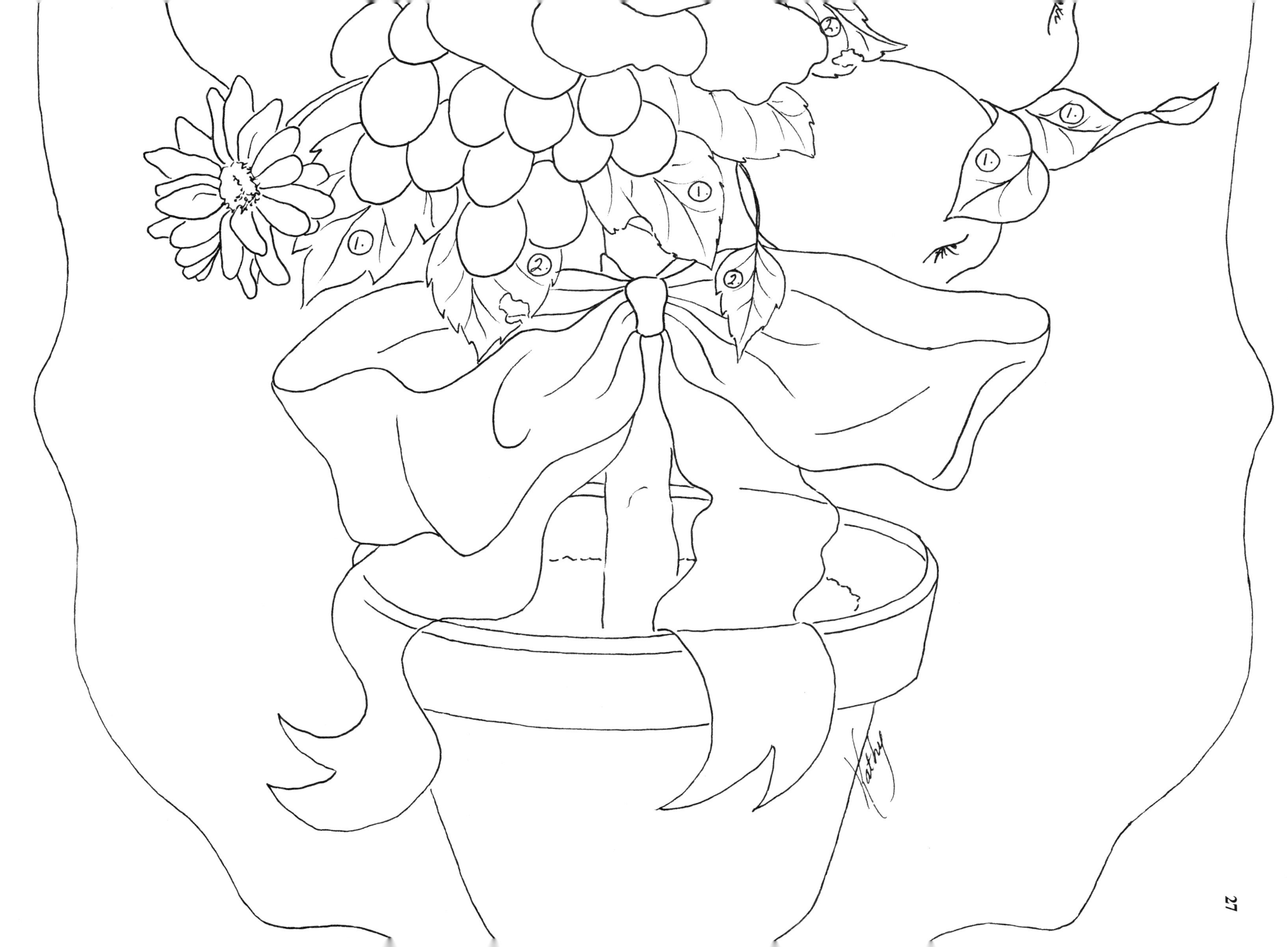

Topiary Tree - Antique Pillow
ACRYLIC ON FABRIC

SUPPLIES
1 Beige Standard Size Pillow Case with Lace Trim
30 oz. Poly-Fil Polyester Fiber Pillow Filling
Deco Americana Control Medium
Pigma .02 Black Permanent Ink Pen (optional brand)

4 Tea Bags
Several Rubber Bands
Light Box (optional)

BRUSHES
Fabric Art Scrubber CB-72
Fabric Art Soft CB-73 (flat)
1/8 White Dove 660 (Deerfoot)

Fabric Art Soft CB-71 (round)
Fabric Art Liner CB-7 (liner)

PALETTE - <u>Deco Americana Acrylics</u>

RED VIOLET	COUNTRY BLUE	BABY PINK
BLACK PLUM	MIDNITE GREEN	GREEN MIST
LIGHT BUTTERMILK	HONEY BROWN	ALIZARIN CRIMSON
HAUSER MED GREEN	PRUSSIAN BLUE	BOYSENBERRY
MOON YELLOW		

PREP
1. Gather up sections of fabric, wring tight with your hands and wrap a rubber band around it to hold in place.
2. Boil 4 tea bags in I gallon water. Carefully submerge tied pillow case into tea water and leave for about 2 minutes. Stir with a wooden spoon.
3. Remove from tea water and rinse out excess tea with cold water (do not rinse out tea bags).
4. Spread pillow case out on flat surface and lay tea bags on it in four differnt areas. Let tea bags sit for 10 minutes. Remove bags and rinse again.
5. Dry fabric in dryer or air dry.
6. Using a light box, transfer the pattern to the fabric, with a Permanent Black Pen.
7. Slip a piece of cardboard into pillowcase. Tape plastic bags to back side of board to keep fabric from getting dirty while painting.

DETAILED INSTRUCTIONS - LIGHT SOURCE - Front
1. First, scrub Control Medium into the area to be painted.
2. Pick up more Medium in your brush before picking up the color indicated.
3. After applying shade color, use the scrubber to blend.

APPLES
1. Apply thinned HAUSER MED. GREEN in some areas of apples.
2. Scrub thinned RED VIOLET into all apple other areas.
3. Shade BLACK PLUM.
4. Highlight with LIGHT BUTTERMILK + •RED VIOLET, sparkle dot is LIGHT BUTTERMILK.
5. When the area is dry, apply 1/2 Control Medium + 1/2 ALIZARIN CRIMSON over RED VIOLET areas of apples (allow to streak somewhat).

DAISIES
1. Scrub in LIGHT BUTTERMILK on all petals.
2. Fill in center with MOON YELLOW.
3. Shade with HONEY BROWN and deepen with HONEY BROWN + BLACK PLUM.

RIBBON AND BOW
1. Scrub in COUNTRY BLUE.
2. Shade with thinned PRUSSIAN BLUE and deepen with same.
3. Highlight with LIGHT BUTTERMILK.
4. Accent with RED VIOLET.

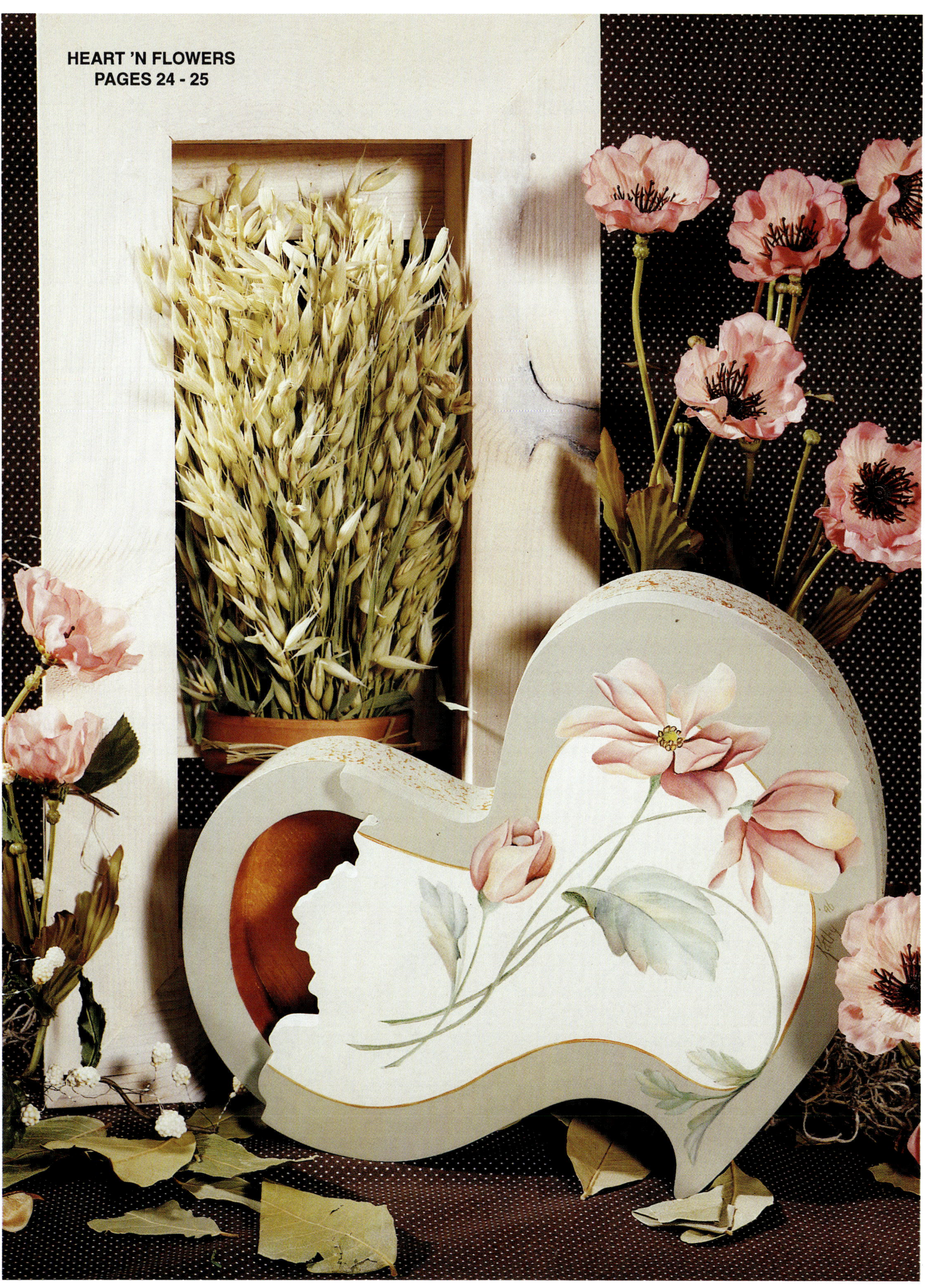

HEART 'N FLOWERS
PAGES 24 - 25

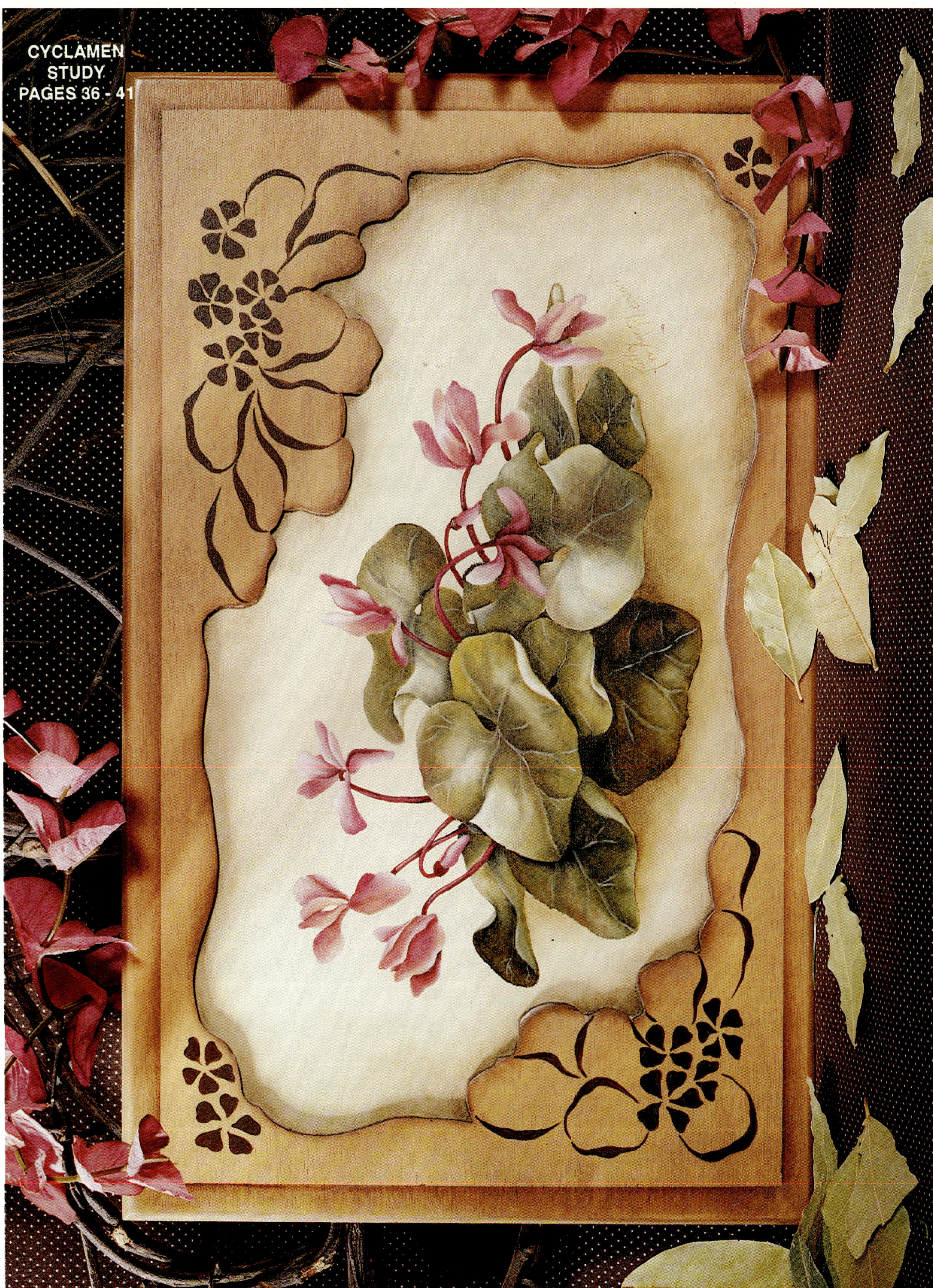

CYCLAMEN
STUDY
PAGES 36 - 41

TOPIARY TREE - ANTIQUE PILLOW continued

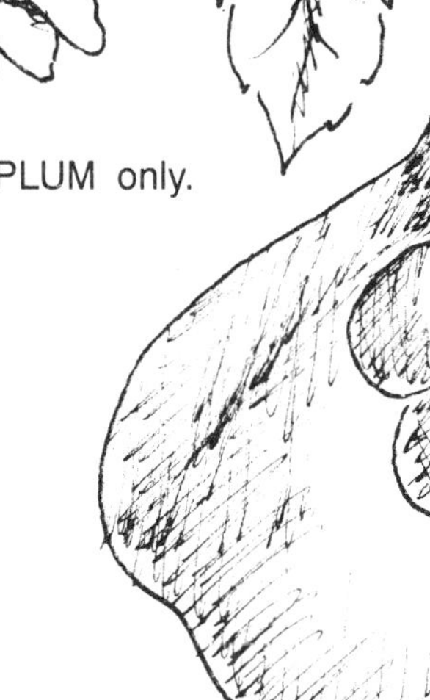

ROSES AND BUDS
I. Scrub in BABY PINK on all roses.
2. Tip each petal with BOYSENBERRY.
3. Shade with BABY PINK + BLACK PLUM, deepen with BLACK PLUM only.
4. Highlight with LIGHT BUTTERMILK.
5. Accent with COUNTRY BLUE.

PLUMS
I. Scrub in BLACK PLUM + LIGHT BUTTERMILK on all plums.
2. Shade with BLACK PLUM.
3. Highlight with mix 1. (above) and more LIGHT BUTTERMILK.
4. Accent with COUNTRY BLUE.

RED GRAPES
I. Scrub in RED VIOLET on all red grapes.
2. Shade on left with thinned PRUSSIAN BLUE.
3. Shade in deep areas and background with BLACK PLUM.
4. Highlight with LIGHT BUTTERMILK + RED VIOLET, then LIGHT BUTTERMILK only, for sparkle shine.

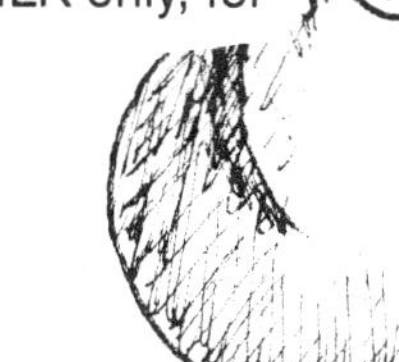

PURPLE GRAPES
I. Scrub in thinned ALIZARIN CRIMSON.
2. Shade on left with thinned PRUSSIAN BLUE.
3. Deep shading & background are PRUSSIAN BLUE.
4. Highlight with WHITE + ALIZARIN CRIMSON, then LIGHT BUTTERMILK only for sparkle shine.

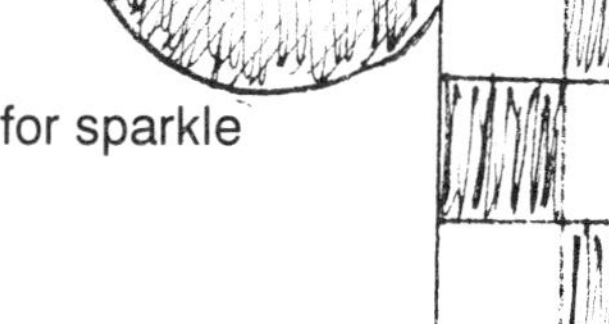

PEARS
I. Scrub in thinned ALIZARIN CRIMSON in some areas.
2. Shade with thinned MIDNITE GREEN at edges and flip-float at neck area.
3. Deepen shade with MIDNITE GREEN.
4. Highlight with MOON YELLOW + LIGHT BUTTERMILK, sparkle shine is LIGHT BUTTER-MILK only.

TRUNK
I. Scrub in LIGHT BUTTERMILK + HONEY BROWN + •BLACK PLUM.
2. Shade with BLACK PLUM + HONEY BROWN.

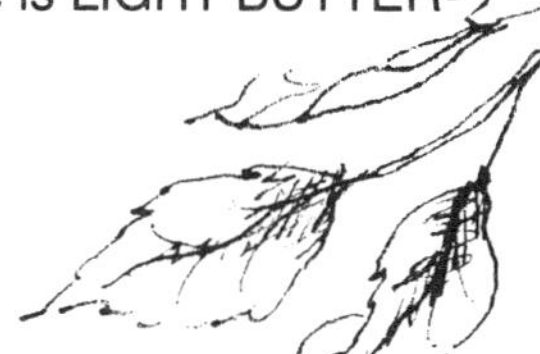

CLAY POT
1. Shade with BOYSENBERRY at left and right edges, moving toward the right center and lightening as you go. Right center should have no paint (highlight).
2. Repeat first step with BLACK PLUM (but not coming to the center quite as far).
3. Cast shadows and under rim are BLACK PLUM.

ROSE LEAVES (jagged edged leaves)
I. Scrub in GREEN MIST.
2. Shade MIDNITE GREEN at base and down main vein line. Deepen with same at overlaps and for cast shadows.
3. Highlight with LIGHT BUTTERMILK + MOON YELLOW + GREEN MIST.
4. Accent with ALIZARIN CRIMSON and then COUNTRY BLUE.

OTHER LEAVES - (smooth edged leaves)
I. Scrub in 3 parts MOON YELLOW + I part GREEN MIST mixed.
2. Follow instructions from #2-4 for Rose Leaves.

TOPIARY TREE - ANTIQUE PILLOW continued

FINISHING

1. Border check design is drawn with a Permanent Black Pen by measuring off 2 rows of l" squares on all 4 sides of the pillowcase.
2. Paint every other square l/2 COUNTRY BLUE + 1/2 CONTROL MEDIUM. Let dry.
3. Apply a coat of CONTROL MEDIUM over each painted square and then shade PRUSSIAN BLUE at left side.
4. Measure out l/4" from the outside edge of the checked border. Paint this area l/2 BOYSEN-BERRY, 1/2 CONTROL MEDIUM. Dry.
5. Apply a coat of CONTROL MEDIUM, then shade at outside edge with BLACK PLUM.
6. Remove all plastic bags and tape.
7. Iron pillowcase to heat set the paint and to remove any wrinkles.
8. Fill with pillow stuffing and tie with ribbons of your choice.

"SUMMER BOUNTY" PLATTER

OIL

PALETTE -

Deco Americana Acrylics

BUTTERMILK	LT. AVOCADO	GOLDEN STRAW

Winsor & Newton Oils

TITANIUM WHITE	CADMIUM YELLOW PALE	BURNT UMBER
COBALT BLUE	CADMIUM RED	BLACK
ALIZARIN CRIMSON	TERRE VERDE GREEN	

PREP

1. Base entire platter BUTTERMILK.
2. "Scumble" (see Terms) the outside frame area with BUTTERMILK + LT. AVOCADO + •GOLDEN STRAW. Also, scumble the back border area.
3. Transfer the patterns for the inset and the border LIGHTLY.
4. Use a 1/0 liner and LT. AVOCADO to line the border comma design.

DETAILED INSTRUCTIONS - LIGHT SOURCE - Upper left side

PEARS

Medium Value -	3 parts CADMIUM YELLOW + 1 part WHITE + •BURNT UMBER
Light Value -	1 part Medium Value + 1 part WHITE
Highlight Value -	WHITE + •Light Value
Dark Value -	2 parts Medium Value + 1 part BURNT UMBER
Very Dark Value -	2 parts Dark Value + 1 part BURNT UMBER
Accent -	Apple Dark Value

APPLES

Medium Value -	3 parts WHITE + 2 parts CADMIUM RED + 1 part ALIZ. CRIMSON
Light Value -	1 part Medium Value + 1 part WHITE
Highlight Value -	WHITE + •Light Value
Dark Value -	1 part Medium Value + 1 part ALIZARIN CRIMSON + •BURNT UMBER
Very Dark Value -	ALIZARIN CRIMSON + •BURNT UMBER
Accent -	Plum Medium Value

PLUMS

Medium Value -	1 part COBALT BLUE + 1 part WHITE + 1 part Apple Medium Value
Light Value -	1 part WHITE + 1 part Medium Value
Highlight Value -	WHITE + •Light Value
Dark Value -	2 parts Medium Value + 1 part BLACK
Very Dark Value -	2 parts COBALT BLUE + 1 part BLACK + 1 part ALIZARIN CRIMSON
Accent -	Apple Medium Value

SUMMER BOUNTY PLATTER continued

GREEN GRAPES

Medium Value -	2 parts CADMIUM YELLOW + 2 parts WHITE + •BLACK
Light Value -	1 part Medium Value + 1 part WHITE
Highlight Value -	WHITE + •Light Value
Dark Value -	2 parts Medium Value + 1 part BURNT UMBER
Very Dark Value -	1 part Dark Value + 1 part BURNT UMBER + •BLACK

PURPLE GRAPES

Medium Value -	2 parts WHITE + 1 part COBALT BLUE + •Apple Medium Value
Light Value -	1 part Medium Value + 1 part WHITE
Highlight Value -	WHITE + • Light Value
Dark Value -	1 part Medium Value + 1 part COBALT BLUE + 1 part ALIZ. CRIMSON
Very Dark Value -	1 part COBALT BLUE + 1 part ALIZARIN CRIMSON + •BLACK

STRAWBERRIES

Medium Value -	3 parts CADMIUM RED + 1 part Green Grape Med. V + •ALIZ. CRIMSON
Light Value -	1 part Medium Value + 1 part WHITE
Highlight Value -	WHITE + • Light Value
Dark Value -	1 part Medium Value + 1 part ALIZARIN CRIMSON + •BURNT UMBER
Very Dark Value -	Apple Very Dark Value

DAISIES

The daisies are white with shade colors of Purple Grape Values. The daisy centers are Pear Values
The accent is Pear Medium Value.

BERRIES

These are Purple Grape Values.

#1 LEAVES

Medium Value -	3 parts CAD YELLOW + 1 part BLACK + 1 part COBALT BLUE + •WHITE
Light Value -	1 part Medium Value + 1 part WHITE
Very Dark Value -	Medium Value + •COBALT BLUE + •BLACK

#2 LEAVES -   Add CADMIUM YELLOW to all #1 Leaves Values

#3 LEAVES -   These leaves are very pale. They are Green Grape Medium to Highlight Values. Accent on all leaves is Strawberry Light Value.

BRANCH -   Use a combination of all leaf values + BURNT UMBER.

FINISHING -   Be sure to accent each piece of fruit with a color that reflects from the adjoining object.

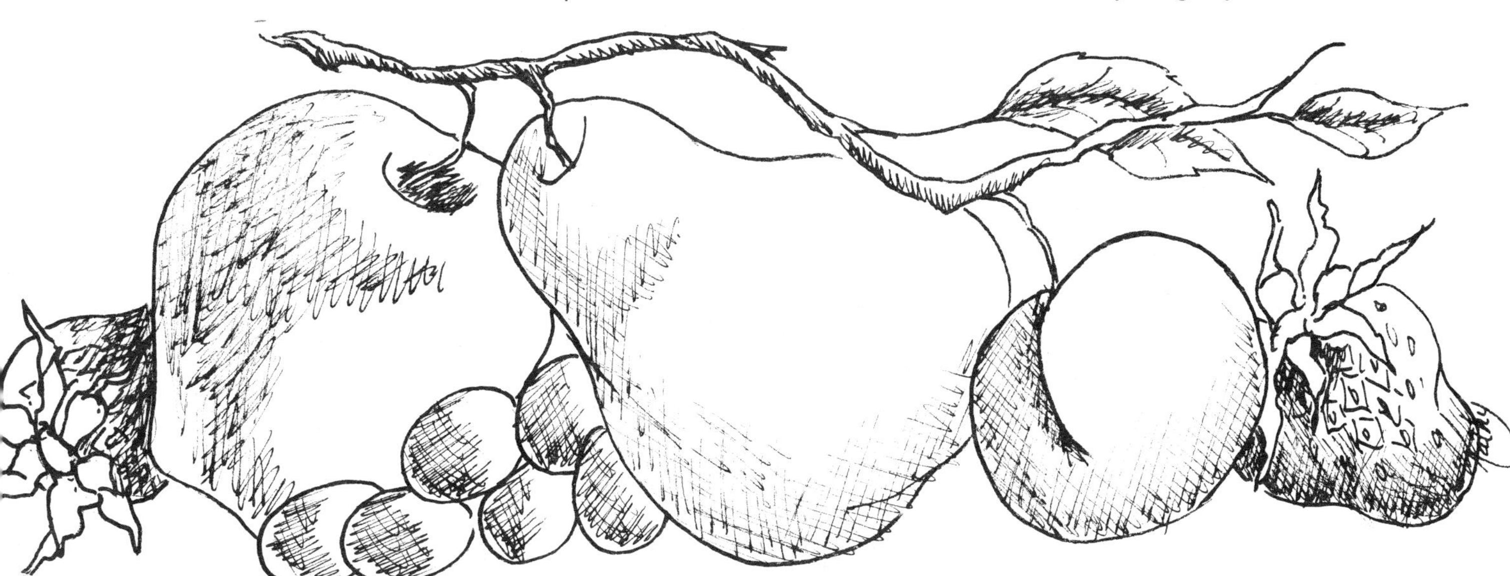

SUMMER BOUNTY PLATTER

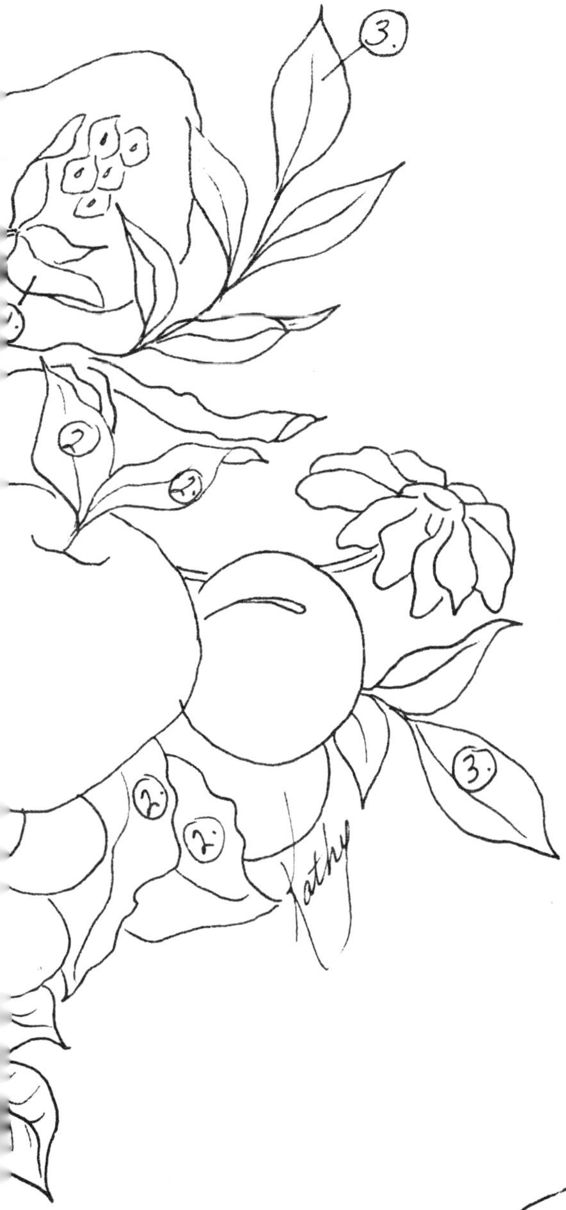

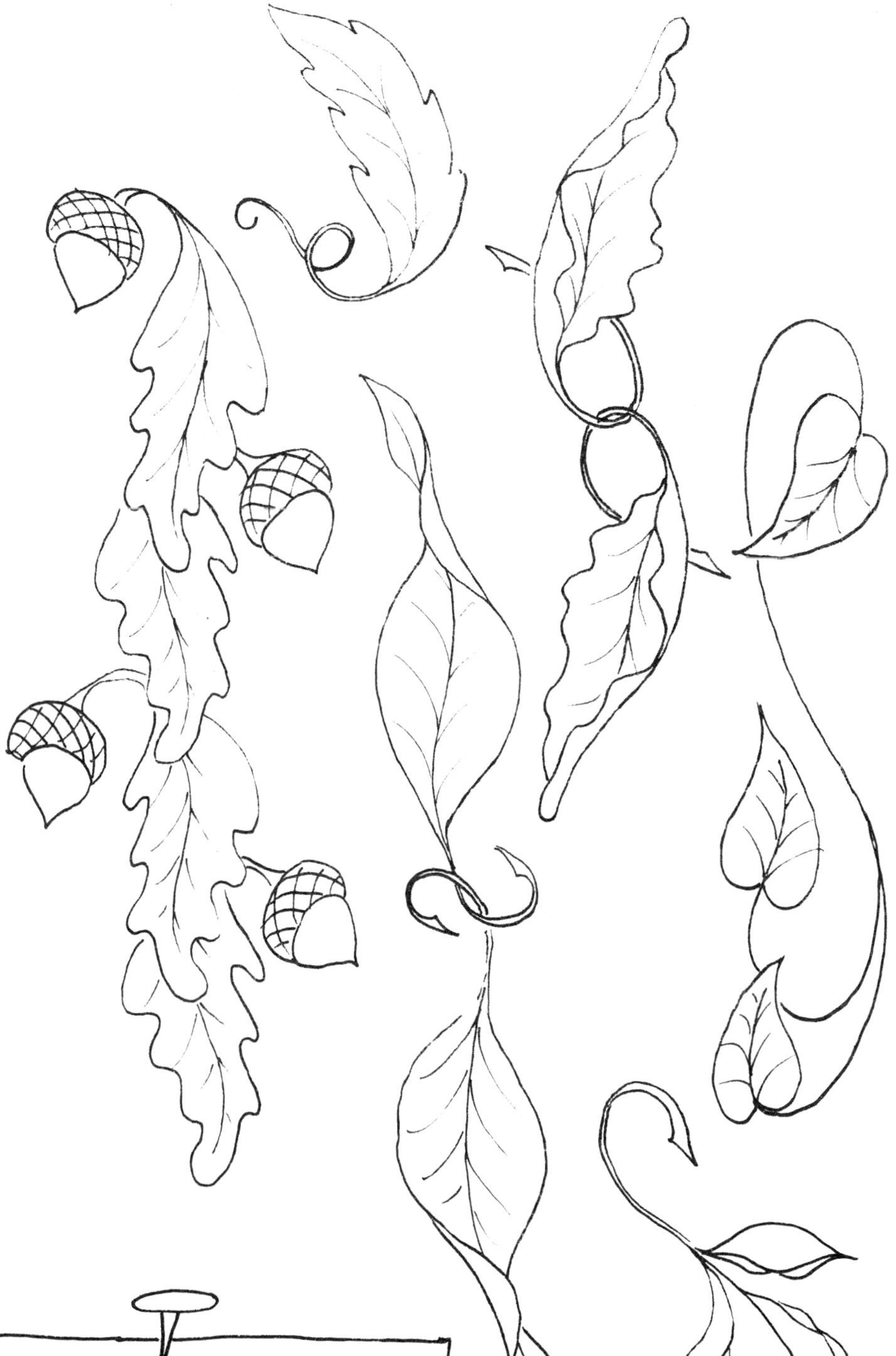

3.

2.

2.

3.

2.

2.

Kathy

Painting Tip

<u>*Want to change or add something in a*</u>
<u>*design but don't know how it will look?*</u>
Here is a great way to see how it will look
without actually applying paint to your
piece: Place a sheet of cellophane (a page
protector works great for this) over your
design. Transfer the new design with a fine
line marker and then paint directly on the
cellophane. When you have finished, simply
wipe off the paint with a wet paper towel.
You can use it over and over.

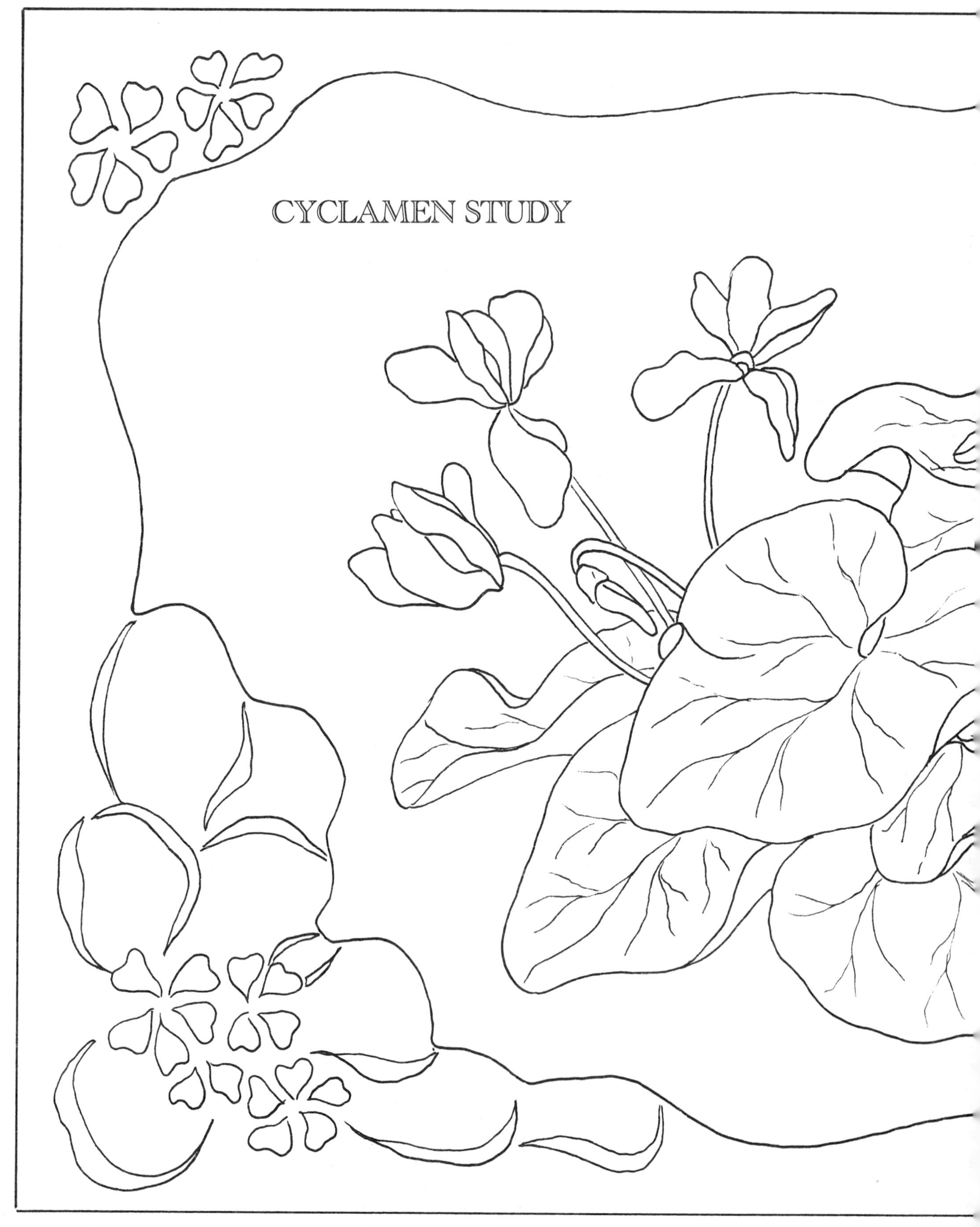
CYCLAMEN STUDY

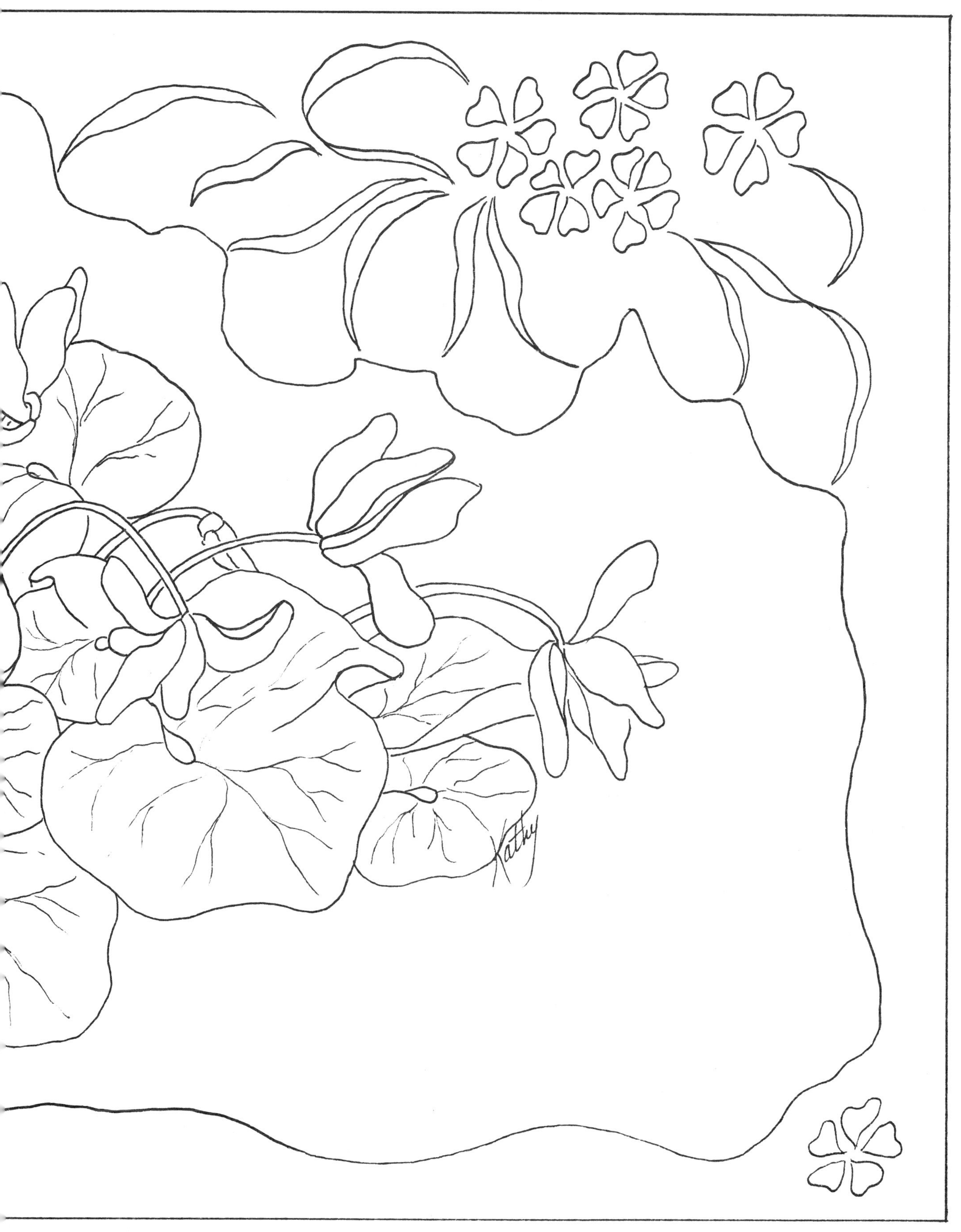
Kathy

CYCLAMEN STUDY

OIL

SUPPLIES Scotch Magic Tape
Extender
Krylon Matte Spray #1311

PALETTE - **Deco Americana Acrylics**

SABLE BROWN	RAW UMBER	TOFFEE
BURNT UMBER		

Winsor & Newton Oils **Shiva**

TITANIUM WHITE	ALIZARIN CRIMSON	PERMASOL RED
CADMIUM YELLOW PALE	BURNT UMBER	PERMASOL
IVORY BLACK		GOLDEN OCHRE

PREP

1. Thin SABLE BROWN and apply wash to entire outer frame. Let dry completely.
2. Position tape 1/2" in from curved outer edge to inside of piece on all four sides.
   Float BURNT UMBER along edge of tape.
3. Base inset TOFFEE.
4. Transfer the pattern for sillouette design.
5. Base sillouette cut-outs BURNT UMBER, line with same.
6. Apply extender at inset edges and float RAW UMBER all the way around. Mop to soften.
7. Transfer pattern for main design on inset.

DETAILED INSTRUCTIONS - LIGHT SOURCE - Upper left front

LEAVES -

Medium Value -	2 parts CADMIUM YELLOW + 2 parts BLACK + 1 part WHITE
Light Value -	1 part Medium Value + 1 part WHITE
Highlight Value -	WHITE + •Light Value
Dark Value -	BLACK + • Medium Value
Very Dark Value -	Dark Value + •BLACK
Accent -	PERMOSOL RED & GOLDEN OCHRE
Vein Lines -	Highlight Value + •BURNT UMBER

1. Concentrate most of the light and highlight values in the center of interest area.
2. This type of plant has leaves that are " fuzzy" or that have tiny hairs all over them. To simulate these leaves, apply the values, but use a pouncing motion (up and down) with small mop brush. Do not swipe across the paint to blend values together, as usual.
3. Keep the darker value on the bottom leaves and also, work down the middle of the leaves... Apply the vein lines (making sure the lines are broken (for interest). Carefully, dab the Dark and Low Dark Values along each side of some vein lines and mop to blend and soften.
4. Use Light and Highlight Values on those leaves that have flips (the underside of the leaf shows).
5. Mist lightly with Matte Spray. When dry, apply the Accent colors. Permosol GOLDEN OCHRE is concentrated on the middle three leaves. The other accent colors are spread throughout the leaves.

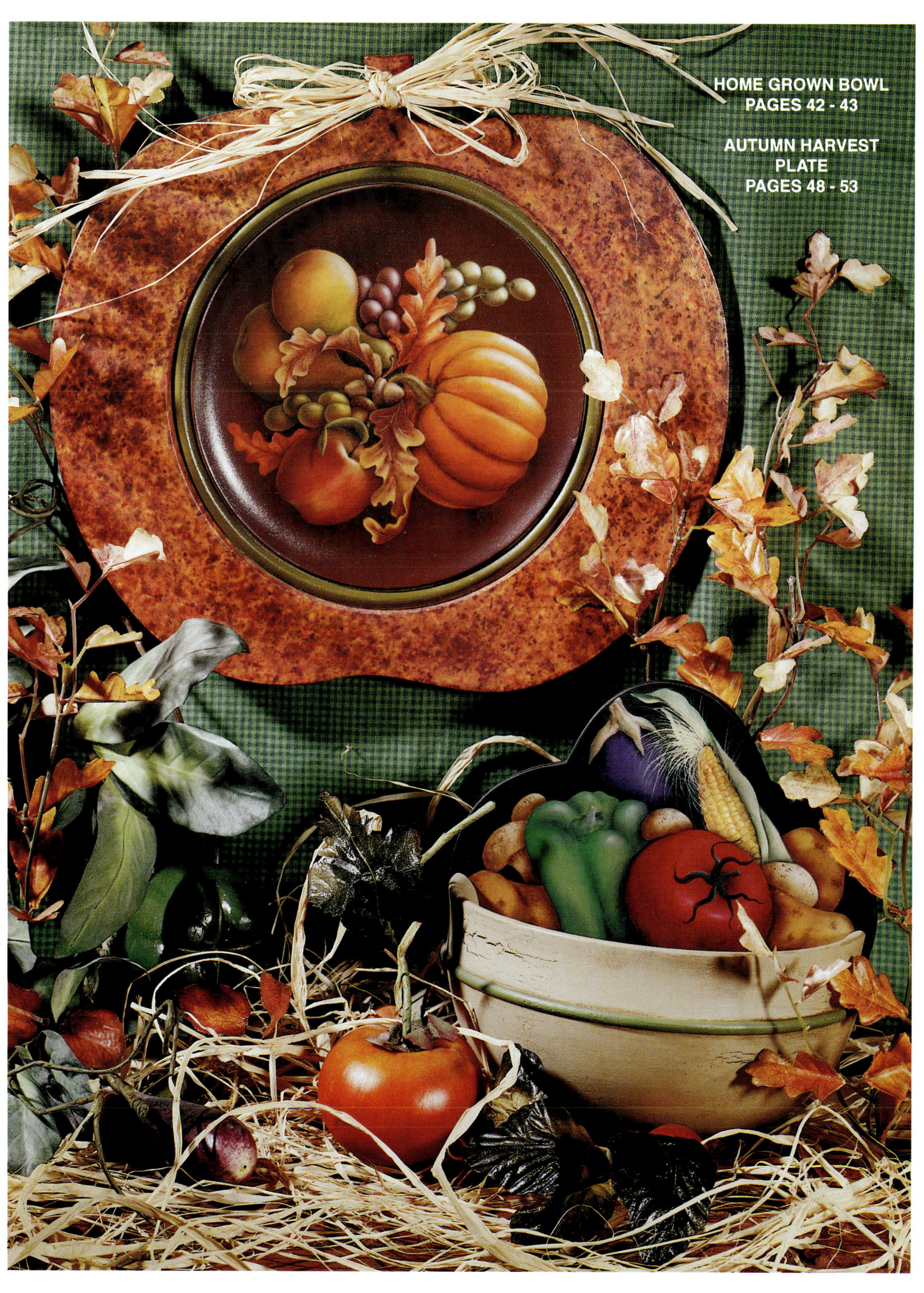
HOME GROWN BOWL
PAGES 42 - 43

AUTUMN HARVEST
PLATE
PAGES 48 - 53

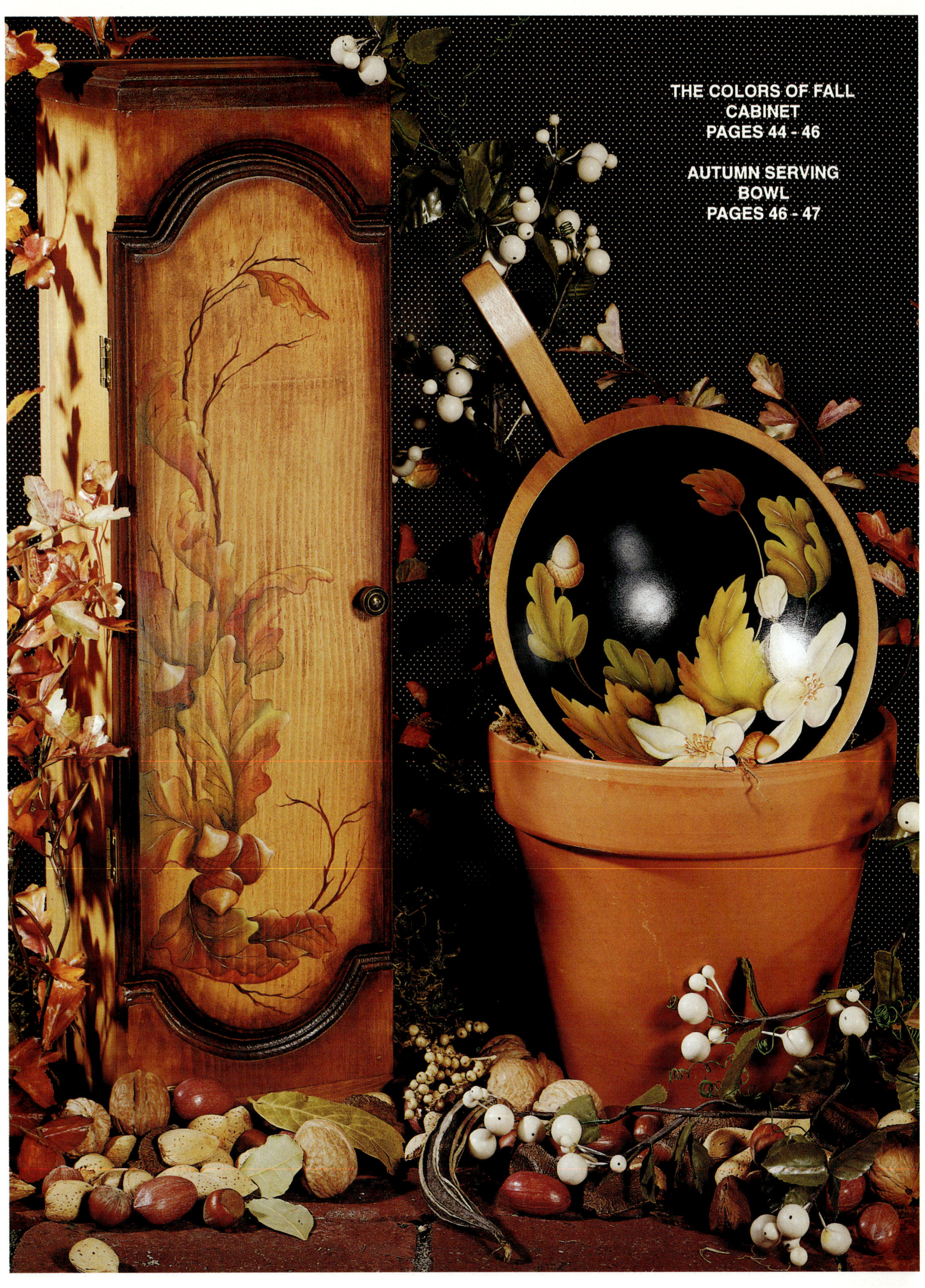

THE COLORS OF FALL
CABINET
PAGES 44 - 46

AUTUMN SERVING
BOWL
PAGES 46 - 47

CYCLAMEN STUDY continued

FLOWERS & STEMS

Medium Value -	1 part ALIZARIN CRIMSON + 1 part WHITE
Light Value -	1 part WHITE + 1 part Medium Value
Highlight Value -	WHITE + •Light Value
Accent -	BURNT UMBER + •Leaves Medium Value

1. Apply the different values and smooth with a mop brush. Use regular sweeping motions for this.
2. Concentrate most of the light and highlight values in "center of interest" area.
3. Lower the intensity of the flowers outside the "center of interest"by applying the Accent value to most of the petals after misting with Krylon Matte.
4. The stems are mainly the Dark Value with shading at both sides of the Low Dark Value. Highlight in the middle of the stems.

BACKGROUND

1. Add a touch of the Leaves Dark Value to BURNT UMBER and thin. Apply at lower half of the flowers, behind the leaves. Soften with a mop.

FINISHING

Follow regular finishing procedures as outlined in TERMS AND INFORMATION.

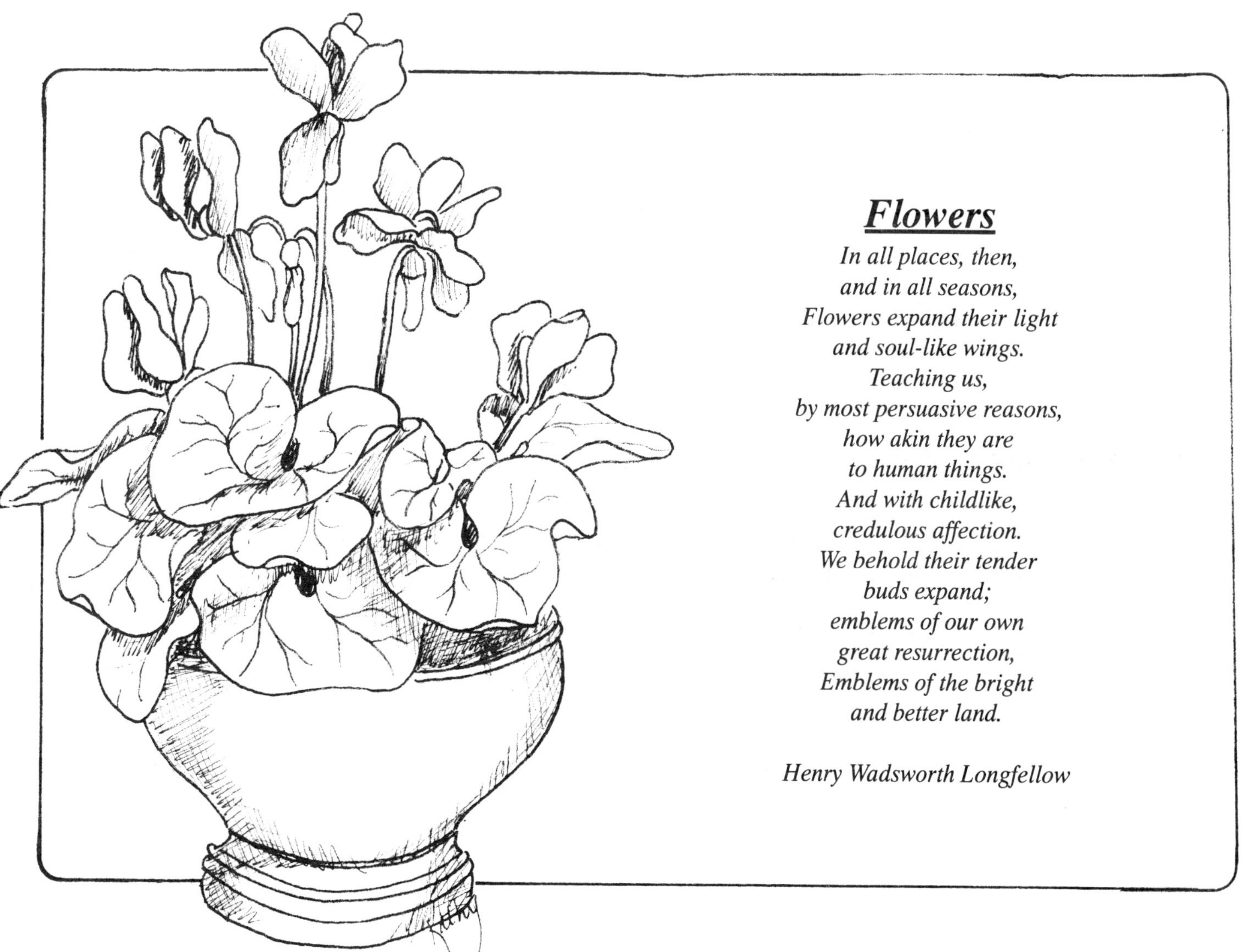

"Home Grown" Bowl
ACRYLIC

SUPPLIES
- DecoArt "Weathered Wood"   Krylon Matte Spray #1311
  Absorbent Paper Towel or Soft Cloth

PALETTE - <u>Deco Americana Acrylics</u>

BLACK	HONEY BROWN	FOREST GREEN
KHAKI TAN	JADE GREEN	MIDNITE GREEN
LIGHT AVOCADO	GOLDEN STRAW	CHARCOAL GREY
BURNT UMBER	RUSSET	BURNT SIENNA
DIOXAZINE PURPLE	BLACK PLUM	LT. BUTTERMILK
PRIMARY RED		

PREP

1. Remove the screws from the back piece.
2. Base both curved half bowl and back piece BLACK.
3. Apply "WEATHERED WOOD" to a couple of areas on half bowl only (apply a thin coat so that cracks will be small). Let dry.
4. Brush on KHAKI TAN over entire half bowl. Be careful applying it over the crackle medium. You can go back and apply a second coat over thin areas (except where crackle medium is).
5. Base the round routed bead and the small routed edge at the bottom of bowl LT. AVOCADO.
6. Spray bowl with MATTE SPRAY. Brush on BURNT UMBER with a large brush over the entire half bowl and with a very lightly damp paper towel or cloth, wipe off (let it remain in the cracks).
7. After the piece has dried completely, transfer the basic pattern lines for the back piece (don't transfer the corn silk, tomato leaves or bell pepper center, yet).
8. Base these opaque -

Green Pepper	LT. AVOCADO
Egg Plant	DIOXAZINE PURPLE
Tomato	PRIMARY RED
Potato	HONEY BROWN
Mushtroom	KHAKI TAN
Corn Husk	JADE GREEN
Corn	GOLDEN STRAW

9. Transfer the detailed pattern for each vegetable.

DETAILED INSTRUCTIONS - LIGHT SOURCE - Front Right

TOMATO

1. Shade to the left with RUSSET (use a flip-float). Shade the middle or core area, also.
2. Highlight with PRIMARY RED + LT. BUTTERMILK. Let dry. Highlight again with LT. AVO-CADO only.
3. Transfer the pattern for the stem and leaves. Base MIDNITE GREEN, highlight by adding a little LT. BUTTERMILK

BELL PEPPER

1. Shade first, with FOREST GREEN, next with MIDNITE GREEN (use a flip-float & mop).
2. Add center stem by floating MIDNITE GREEN at edges, then float MIDNITE GREEN + LT. BUTTERMILK.
3. Highlight with LT. BUTTERMILK on each curved hump.

HOME GROWN BOWL continued

43

"HOME GROWN" BOWL continued
EGG PLANT
1. Highlight by adding LT. BUTTERMILK to DIOXAZINE PURPLE. Flip-float to middle right side.
2. Float BLACK to shade behind other vegetables, behind stem and to each side.
3. The stem is shaded with CHARCOAL GREY and thinned FOREST GREEN.

MUSHROOMS
1. Shade to the left with BURNT UMBER.
2. Highlight to the right with LT. BUTTERMILK.
3. Use an old scruffy brush to dot the top of each mushroom with BURNT UMBER.

CORN
1. Use a liner brush and BURNT SIENNA to line around each corn kernal. Shade to the left of each kernal with same.
2. Highlight to the right with LT. BUTTERMILK.
3. Float CHARCOAL GREY + •BURNT SIENNA to shade behind tomato and corn husks.
4. Shade the corn husks with FOREST GREEN first, next with MIDNITE GREEN.
5. Line corn silk with JADE GREEN, then some with LT. BUTTERMILK.

POTATOES
1. Shade the left side and around the outside edge of each potato with BURNT SIENNA.
2. The eyes are also BURNT SIENNA.

FINISHING
Follow regular finishing procedures.

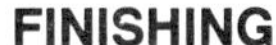

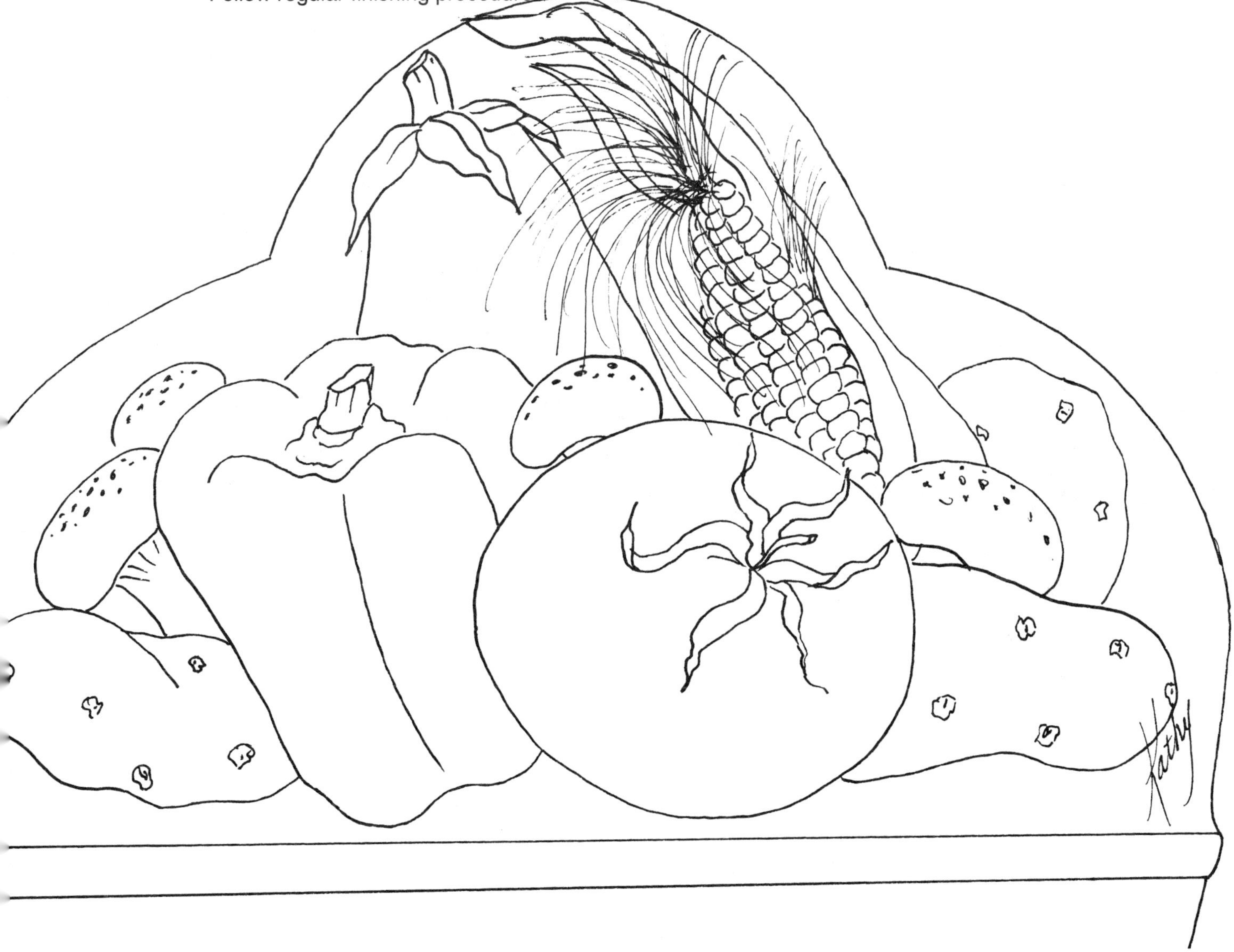

"The Colors Of Fall" Cabinet

Oil

SUPPLIES

Large Flat Brush   Absorbent Paper Towels or Soft Rag

PALETTE - <u>Deco Americana Acrylic</u>

MILK CHOCOLATE   BURNT UMBER

<u>Winsor & Newton Oils</u>

COBALT BLUE   BLACK   CADMIUM YELLOW PALE
ALIZARIN CRIMSON   RAW SIENNA   CADMIUM RED
BURNT UMBER   WHITE

PREP

1. Stain the entire wood cabinet by brushing on a mixture of 2/3 MILK CHOCOLATE + 1/3 BURNT UMBER acrylics, thinned to a watery consistency (brush on & wipe off with cloth or paper towel. I suggest doing the inside first, back, each side, top and bottom, the front next and the door last).
2. To darken the edges, brush on BURNT UMBER only. Do not dilute in water. Brush on and feather out from the edge. Soften with a paper towel or soft cloth (you can add a little water to the tip of your cloth or towel to aid in smoothing out the paint, if needed).
3. Transfer the pattern lightly.

DETAILED INSTRUCTIONS - LIGHT SOURCE - Upper right

This technique is a dry brush method. Apply each color in small amounts by looking at the photo. Don't worry about the colors touching each other, just apply a small amount and then scrub the colors together until they blend (this will lighten the values somewhat, so you may have to reapply the darkest values again).

To achieve the transparent effect of the leaves, just lightly scrub in some Dark Value Orange where the branches stand behind the leaves.

The branches are lined with Very Dark Orange + Very Dark Green. Line the branches thick at the base and very thin at the ends of twigs.

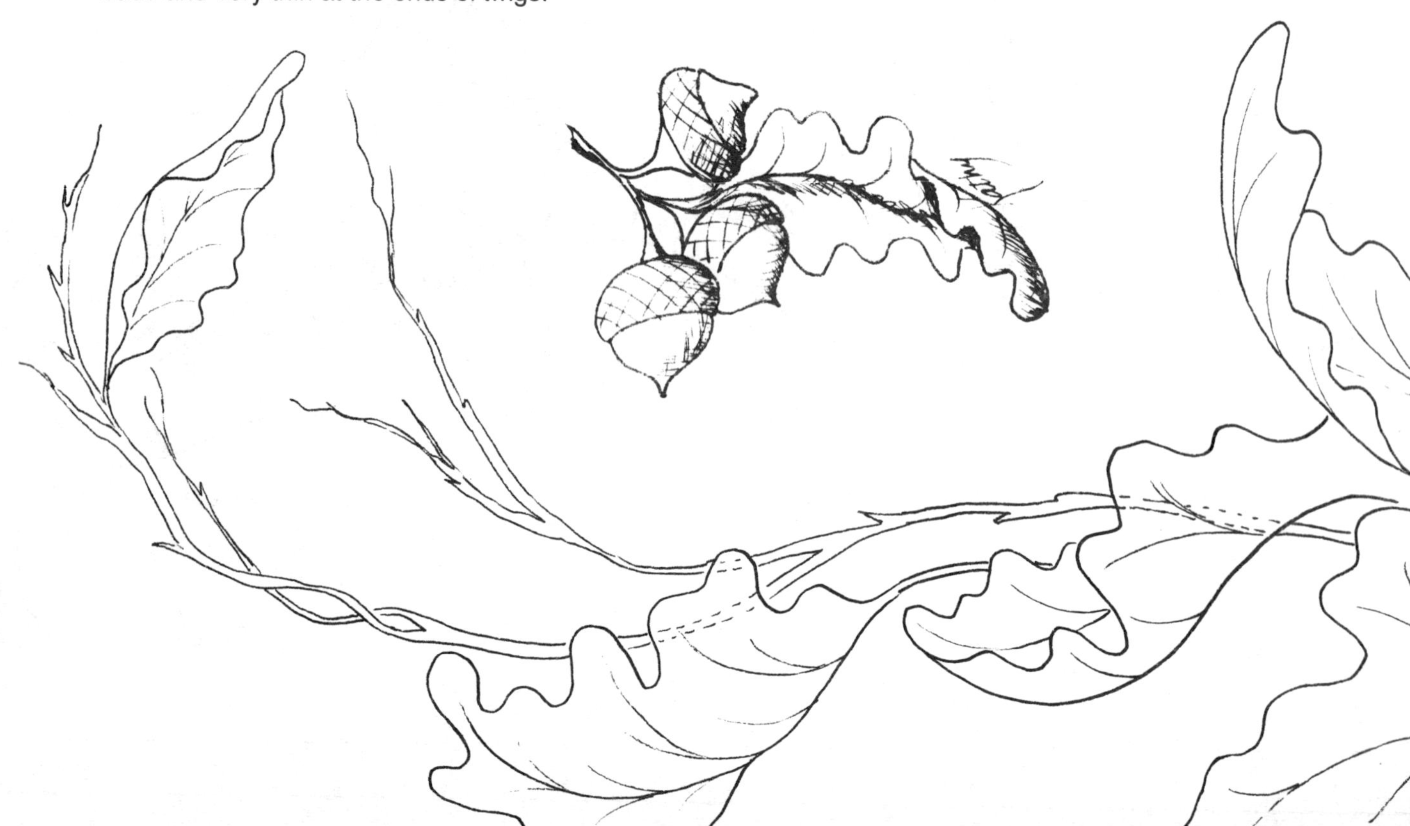

THE COLORS OF FALL CABINET continued

Acorns are crosshatched with Low Dark Orange after the values have been blended together. High light values are added after that.

Vein lines on the leaves are Very Dark Green + Very Dark Orange and are added last. These lines are very thin and whispy. Add Highlight Value where light would hit.

BASIC GREEN -   1 part COBALT BLUE + 1 part and a little more CADMIUM YELLOW PALE.

GREENS

Medium Value -	3 parts Basic Green + 2 parts RAW SIENNA + 1 part CADMIUM YELLOW
Light Value -	1 part Medium Value + 1 part CADMIUM YELLOW
Highlight Value -	WHITE + •Light Value
Dark Value -	1 part Medium Value + 1 part RAW SIENNA
Very Dark Value -	1 part Dark Value + 1 part RAW UMBER + •BLACK

REDS

Medium Value -	3 parts CADMIUM RED + 1 part RAW SIENNA
Light Value -	2 parts Medium Value + 1 part WHITE + •CADMIUM YELLOW
Highlight Value -	WHITE + •Light Value
Dark Value -	1 part Medium Value + 1 part ALIZARIN CRIMSON
Very Dark Value -	2 parts Dark Value + 1 part BURNT UMBER

ORANGES

Medium Value -	3 parts CADMIUM YELLOW + 1 part CADMIUM RED + •WHITE
Light Value -	1 part Medium Value + 1 part CADMIUM YELLOW + • WHITE
Highlight Value -	1 part WHITE + 1 part Light Value
Dark Value -	3 parts Medium Value + 1 part BURNT UMBER
Very Dark Value -	1 part Dark Value + 1 part BURNT UMBER

ACORNS

Medium Value -
3 parts RAW SIENNA + 1part CADMIUM YELLOW
Light Value -
1 part Medium Value + 1 part WHITE
Dark Value -
1 part Oranges Very Dark + 1 part Medium Value

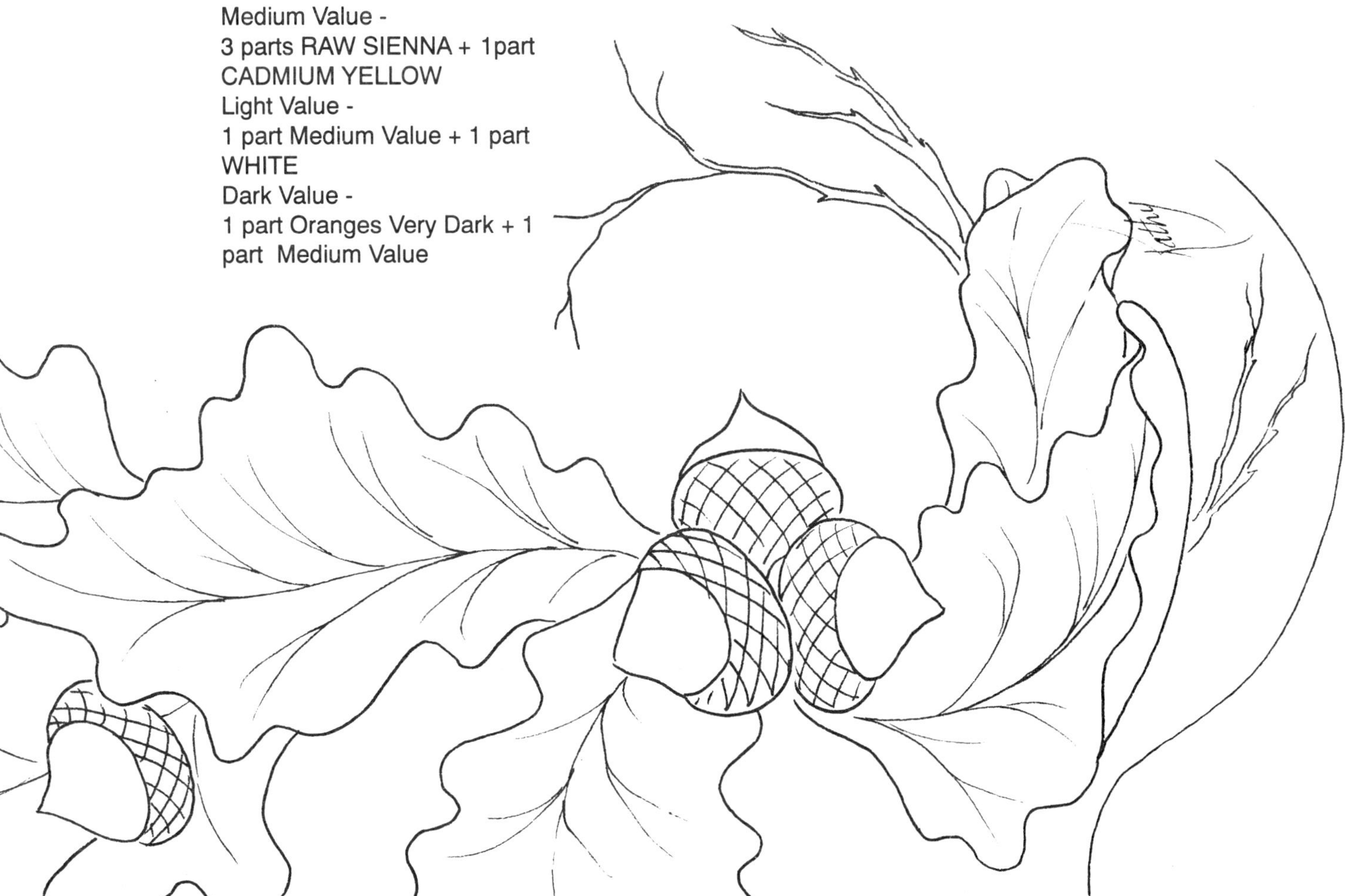

THE COLORS OF FALL CABINET continued

ACORN CAPS

Medium Value -   Oranges Dark Value
Light Value -   WHITE + Medium Value
Dark Value -   Oranges Very Dark

FINISHING

Follow regular finishing procedures. Screw on knob.

AUTUMN SERVING BOWL
ACRYLIC

SUPPLIES -   Extender

PALETTE -   **Deco Americana Acrylics**

RAW SIENNA	YELLOW OCHRE	AVOCADO	BLACK
BERRY RED	BURNT UMBER	ANTIQUE WHITE	

PREP

(Base each item with three thinned coats)

1. Wash the rim and outside of the bowl and the top and bottom of the handle with RAW SIENNA.
2. Base the inside of the bowl and the sides of the handle with BLACK.
3. Transfer the pattern to tracing paper. With scissors, cut along dotted lines (this will enable the pattern to mold to the curved sides of the bowl and make transfering alot easier for you (also, use a small piece of graphite and move it as you transfer the design). Transfer only the basic design now.
4. Base the three flowers ANTIQUE WHITE (remember 3 thinned coats).
5. Base Leaf #1 with 1 part ANTIQUE WHITE + 1 part YELLOW OCHRE mixed.
6. Base Leaf #2 and #6 with 5 parts of the above mix + 1 part BERRY RED mixed.
7. Base Leaf #3 and #4 with 4 parts ANTIQUE WHITE + 4 parts YELLOW OCHRE + 1 part AVOCADO.
8. Add a little more AVOCADO to the above mix and base Leaf #5.
9. Base acorns 1 part RAW SIENNA + 1 part ANTIQUE WHITE.
10. Transfer the detail pattern LIGHTLY.

DETAILED INSTRUCTIONS - LIGHT SOURCE - Above bowl as it sits on table.

Apply extender to the area first, paint and then lightly mop to blend.

ACORNS

1. Float RAW SIENNA at the top of the cap and top of the body. Also, float down the side that is the closest to the center of the bowl.
2. Line curved cross-hatching on cap with BURNT UMBER.
3. Float 1 part RAW SIENNA + 1 part BURNT UMBER mix to seperate the two acorns, behind leaves or petals and to seperate cap from body.
4. Highlight with ANTIQUE WHITE on the body, at side closest to rim of bowl.

FLOWERS

1. Mix 3 parts BURNT UMBER + 1 part BLACK + 4 parts ANTIQUE WHITE. Shade between each petal and fold on each petal.
2. Dot stamens with #2 Leaf mix. Shade them toward side nearest center of bowl.
3. Line the stamens going towards the center of the flower with 1 part BURNT UMBER + 1 part RAW SIENNA.
4. Tint the petals by thinning the paint with extender. Tint with BERRY RED, AVOCADO, then RAW SIENNA.

AUTUMN SERVING BOWL continued
ALL LEAVES

1. Float 3 parts AVOCADO + 1 part BURNT UMBER at the base of each leaf and behind other leaves or petals. Flip-float the same mix down the vein line areas of each leaf.
2. Deepen the shade by adding more BURNT UMBER and shading again behind petals and other leaves
3. Line the veins with ANTIQUE WHITE + Leaf #1 mix.
4. Tint with the same colors as in the flowers.

FINISHING

1. Follow regular finishing procedures.
2. Attach the handle with screws and paint them to match the bowl color.

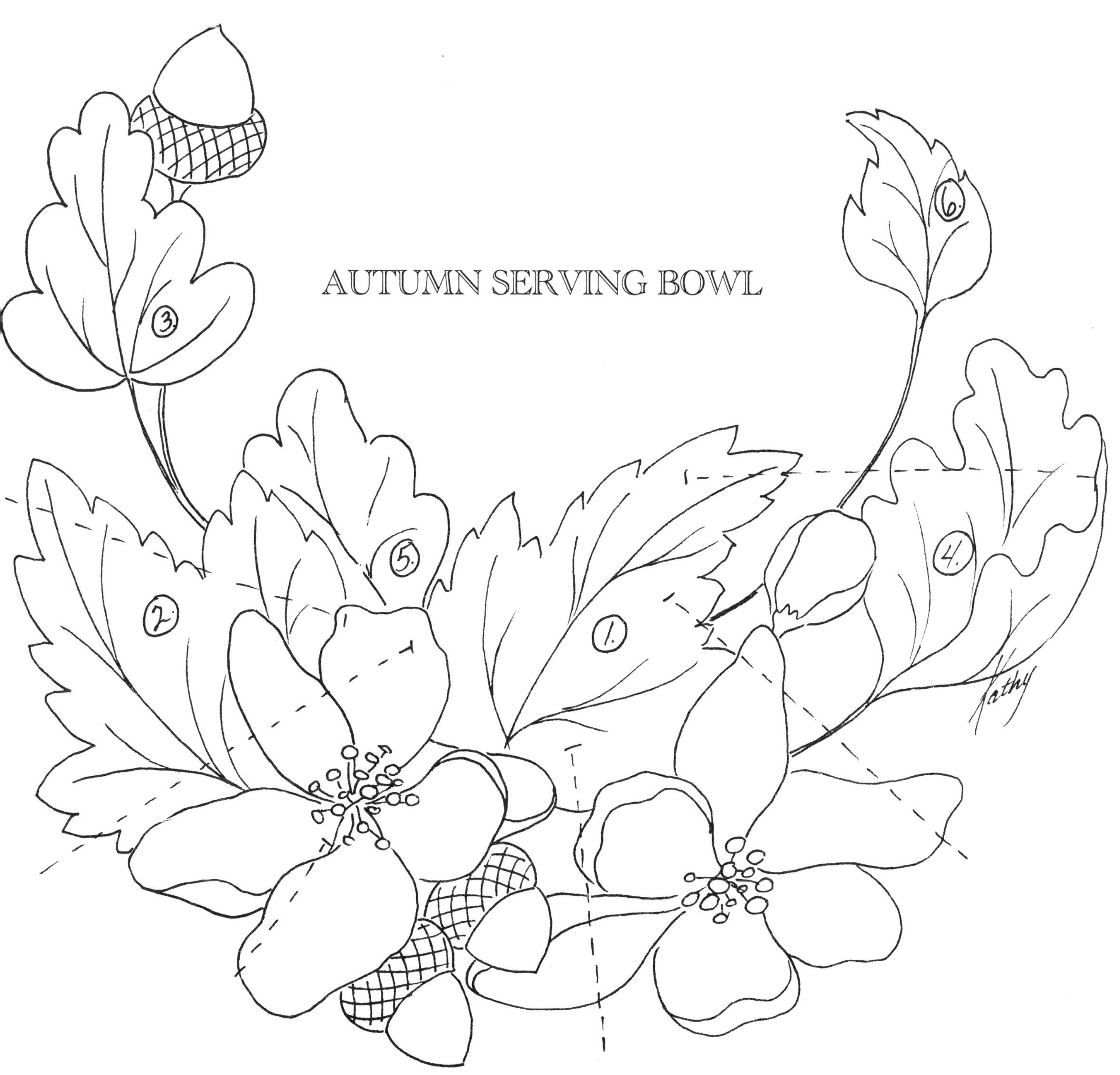

"Autumn Harvest" Plate"

OIL

SUPPLIES

Extender   Plastic Bag   Scruffy Brush

PALETTE - <u>Deco Americana Acrylics</u>

ANTIQUE MAROON	DEEP BURGUNDY	ANTIQUE GREEN
RED IRON OXIDE	TANGERINE	PLUM
HONEY BROWN	NAPTHOL RED	YELLOW OCHRE
BURNT UMBER		

<u>Winsor & Newton Oils</u>

TITANIUM WHITE	ALIZARIN CRIMSON	RAW SIENNA
CADMIUM YELLOW PALE	COBALT BLUE	BLACK
CADMIUM RED	BURNT UMBER	

PREP

1. Base outside the routed circle TANGERINE (sides, too).
2. Apply a liberal coat of extender over the based Tangerine Area. Crumple up a portion of a plastic bag. Dip into BURNT UMBER and pat on palette to remove excess paint. Pounce over the area evenly. Let dry. Repeat this process with DEEP BURGUNDY and then with a mix of 2/3 PLUM + 1/3 BURNT UMBER. (Use a scruffy brush to do this process on the inside edge).
3. Base the routed circle ANTIQUE GREEN.
4. Base the area inside the routed circle ANTIQUE MAROON. Also, base the back.
5. Transfer the basic pattern lines, lightly.

BASING MIXES - BE SURE NOT TO DISTORT THE SHAPES. BASE SMOOTH, WITHOUT CHOPPY BRUSH MARKS. BASE THESE ACRYLIC:

Pumpkin -	TANGERINE
Apple -	NAPTHOL RED
Gourd #1 -	TANGERINE + •BURNT UMBER
Gourd #2 -	Add more BURNT UMBER to above mix
Leaf #1 -	YELLOW OCHRE
Leaves #2 & 3 -	HONEY BROWN
Leaf #4 -	RED IRON OXIDE

COLOR MIXES

PUMPKIN -

Medium Value -	5 parts CAD. YELLOW + 1 part CAD. RED + •BURNT UMBER
Light Value -	3 parts Medium Value + 1 part WHITE
Highlight Value -	WHITE + •Light Value
Dark Value -	3 parts Medium V + 1 part BURNT UMBER + •COBALT BLUE
Very Dark Value -	2 parts BURNT UMBER + 1 part CAD RED + •COBALT BLUE
Accent -	Medium Green Value
Accent -	ALIZARIN CRIMSON

APPLE -

Medium Value -	2 parts CAD RED + 1 part CAD YELLOW + •BURNT UMBER
Medium Light Value -	2 parts WHITE + 1 part Medium Value
Light Value -	Add WHITE to Medium Light + •CAD YELLOW
Highlight Value -	WHITE + •Light Value
Dark Value -	3 parts Medium Value + 1 part BURNT UMBER
Very Dark Value -	1 part Dark Value + 1 part BURNT UMBER + 1 part ALIZ. CRIM.
Accent -	Medium Green Mix

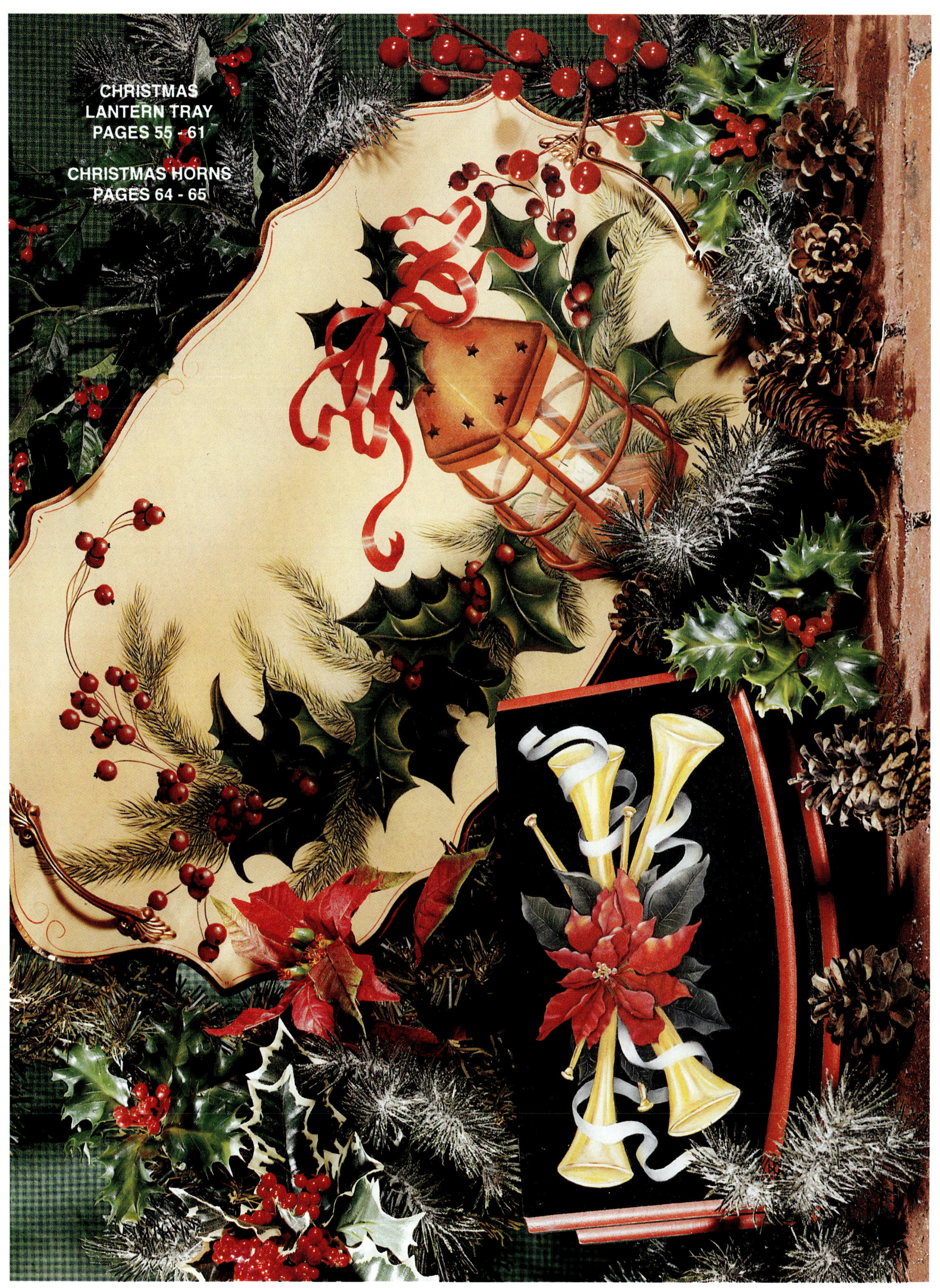

CHRISTMAS
LANTERN TRAY
PAGES 55 - 61

CHRISTMAS HORNS
PAGES 64 - 65

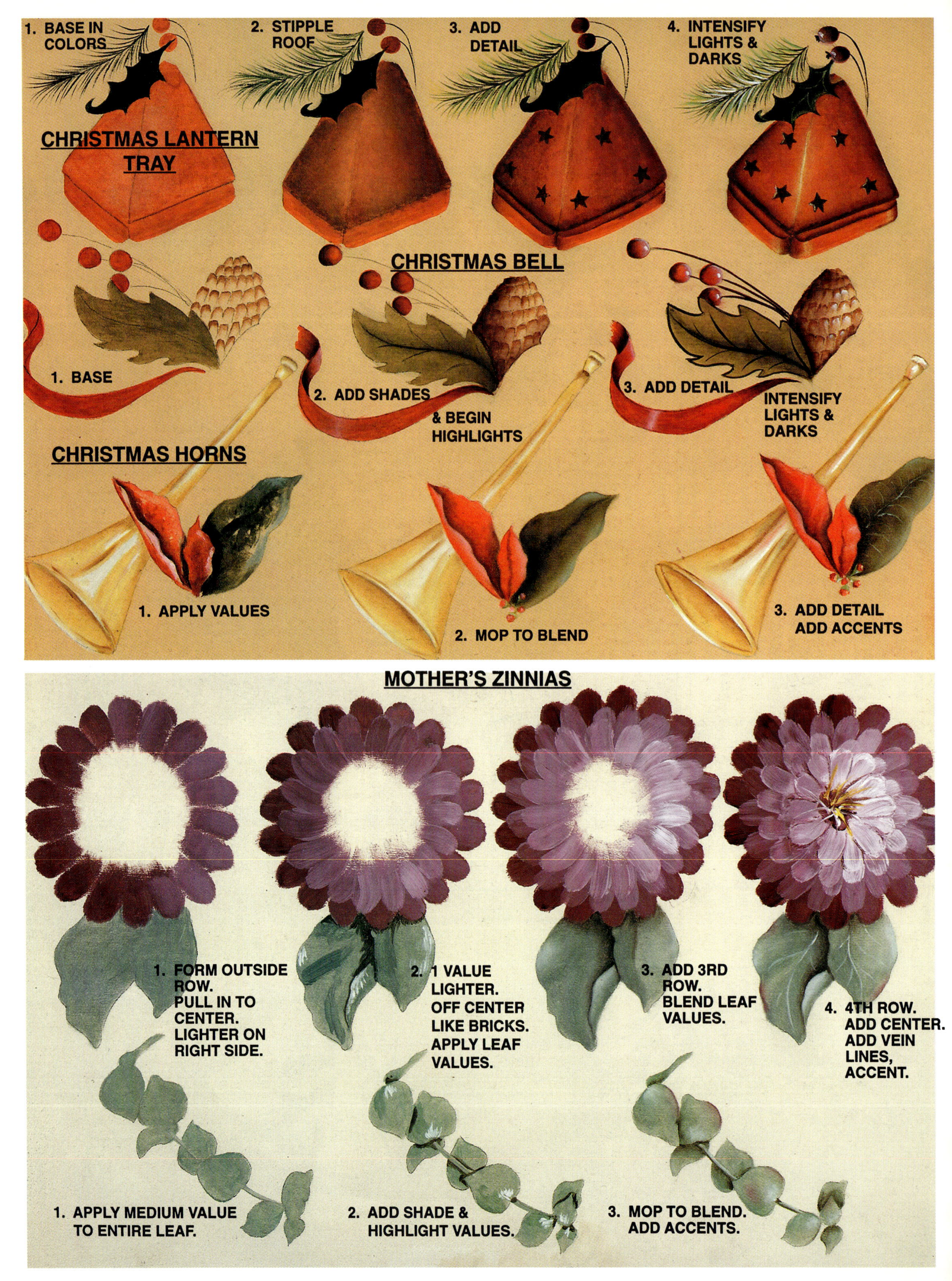

1. BASE IN COLORS
2. STIPPLE ROOF
3. ADD DETAIL
4. INTENSIFY LIGHTS & DARKS

CHRISTMAS LANTERN TRAY

CHRISTMAS BELL

1. BASE
2. ADD SHADES & BEGIN HIGHLIGHTS
3. ADD DETAIL
INTENSIFY LIGHTS & DARKS

CHRISTMAS HORNS

1. APPLY VALUES
2. MOP TO BLEND
3. ADD DETAIL ADD ACCENTS

MOTHER'S ZINNIAS

1. FORM OUTSIDE ROW. PULL IN TO CENTER. LIGHTER ON RIGHT SIDE.
2. 1 VALUE LIGHTER. OFF CENTER LIKE BRICKS. APPLY LEAF VALUES.
3. ADD 3RD ROW. BLEND LEAF VALUES.
4. 4TH ROW. ADD CENTER. ADD VEIN LINES, ACCENT.

1. APPLY MEDIUM VALUE TO ENTIRE LEAF.
2. ADD SHADE & HIGHLIGHT VALUES.
3. MOP TO BLEND. ADD ACCENTS.

AUTUMN HARVEST PLATE continued
APPLE LEAF & STEM -   Use Green Mixes below

GREEN MIXES

Medium Value -   5 parts CAD YELLOW + 1 part COBALT BLUE + •BURNT UMBER
Light Value -   2 parts CAD YELLOW + 1 part Medium Value
Highlight Value -   WHITE + •Light Value
Dark Value -   2 parts Medium Value + 1 part BURNT UMBER
Very Dark Value -   1 part Medium Value + 1 part ALIZARIN CRIMSON + 1 part COBALT BLUE

GOURD #1 -   Top half - Use Green Mix Values.
    Bottom half - Use Pumpkin Values + RAW SIENNA.

GOURD #2 -   Whole gourd - Use Pumpkin Mixes & Green Mix (keep values darker than top gourd)

PURPLE GRAPES

Medium Value -   3 parts CAD RED + 2 parts COB. BLUE + 1 part WHITE + •CAD YELLOW
Light Value -   1 part Medium Value + 1 part WHITE + •CAD YELLOW
Highlight Value -   WHITE + •Light Value
Dark Value -   1 part Medium Value + 1 part ALIZARIN CRIMSON + •CAD YELLOW
Very Dark Value -   1 part ALIZARIN CRIM. + 1 part COBALT BLUE + 1 part CAD YELLOW
Accent -   Medium Green Mixes

GREEN GRAPES

Medium to Very Dark -   Use Green Mixes
Hightlights -   Highlights are the greatest on these grape
Accent -   Pumpkin Light Mix

ACORNS

Medium Value -   BURNT UMBER + WHITE + •CAD YELLOW
Light Value -   Add WHITE
Very Dark Value -   Add BURNT UMBER + •Very Dark Green Value
Crosshatching -   BURNT UMBER
(RIGHT ACORN SHOULD BE LIGHTEST OF THE THREE)

LEAF #4   Outside edge -   CAD RED + •BURNT UMBER
    Inside area -   Pumpkin Medium Value
    Dark Value -   Pumpkin Dark Value
    Very Dark Value -   Pumpkin Very Dark Value
    Vein Lines & Spots -   BURNT UMBER

LEAF #3   Inside area -   Purple Grapes Medium to Very Dark Values
    Outside edge -   Acorn Light VALUE + CAD YELLOW, shade Med. Green Mix
    Highlight by adding WHITE
    Vein Lines & Spots -   BURNT UMBER, then Outside edge Value

LEAF #2   Outside edge -   BURNT UMBER + WHITE + •CADMIUM RED
    Inside area -   Purple Grape Medium to Dark Values
    Vein Lines & Spots -   Purple Grapes Very Dark Value, then Outside edge Value
    Accent -   Green Mixes

LEAF #1   Outside edge -   Pumpkin Medium Value + •ALIZARIN CRIMSON
    Inside area -   Pumpkin Light Values
    Dark Value -   Pumpkin Dark Values
    Vein Lines & Spots -   BURNT UMBER, then Inside area value

BACKGROUND

Should be shaded in LEFT LOWER AREA by adding BLACK to BURNT UMBER. It should have three value changes. All cast shadows should, also, have three value changes.

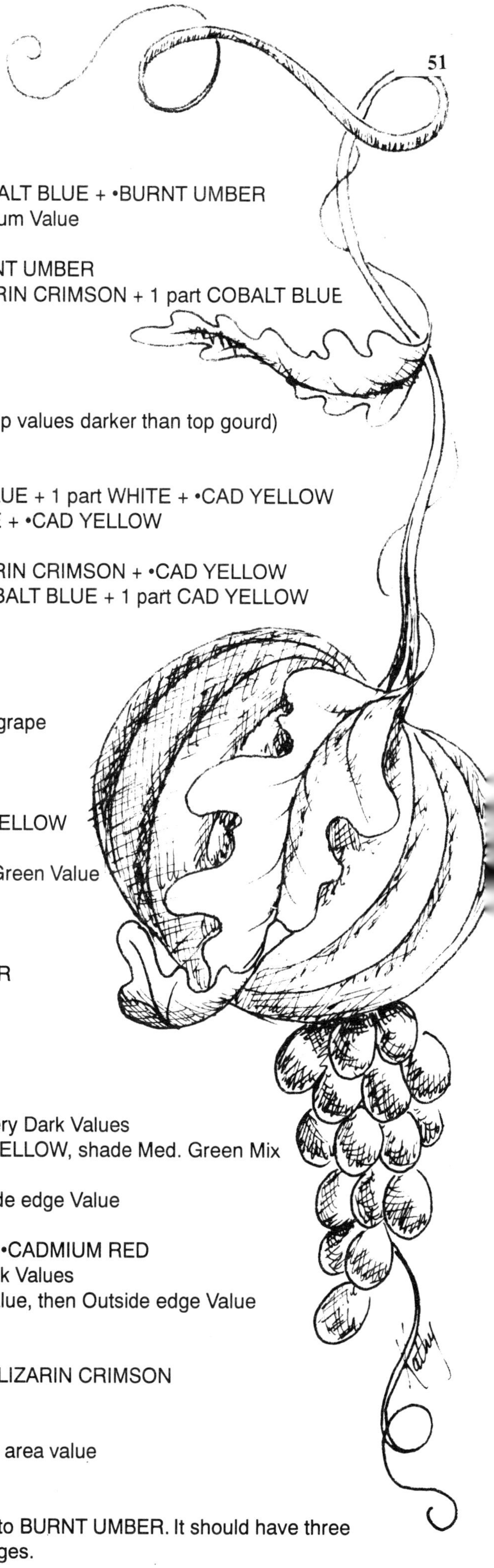

AUTUMN HARVEST PLATE continued
DETAILED INSTRUCTIONS - LIGHT SOURCE - Upper right side
FIRST STAGE

PUMPKIN - Shade to left of each section and in center stem area. Place highlight values to right of each section. You can build additional highlight areas after spraying. The stem is Green Mixes.

APPLE - Lay in Apple Values as indicated on photo. Don't add Green Accent yet. Keep back side of apple very dark. Highlight will be added later. Leaf and stem are Green Values.

GREEN GRAPES -

Lay in Green Values first. Keep shaded areas in a cresent shape. Don't forget reflected light at left side. The lower left grapes between apple and gourd should be darker values than those next to pumpkin (these grapes should receive the, greatest amount of highlight of all the fruit).

GOURD #2 -

Begin with Green Values toward the outside edges, bringing in the Pumpkin Values toward the middle. Keep the values darker than the gourd on top.

GOURD #1-

The bottom half of the gourd is Pumpkin Values, the top half is Green Mix Values. Blend together. Add RAW SIENNA to the top areas.

PURPLE GRAPES- Apply values as you did with the Green Grapes.

ACORNS - The values of the bottom acorn should be the darkest, the one at top right, the lightest.

LEAF #4 - This leaf should have low intensity, but enough color to bring interest to that side of the design.

LEAF #3 - Place outside and inside values as indicated and blend together. Begin to establish ripples (make sure they bend toward the main vein line).

LEAF #2 - Same as Leaf #3.

LEAF #1- This leaf is directly in the path of the light so it should be the brightest. Try to establish transparency by shading where the grapes fall behind the leaf. Begin to establish ripples.

SECOND STAGE - SPRAY MIST WITH KRYLON MATTE SPRAY BEFORE CONTINUING

PUMPKIN - Add an accent of ALIZARIN CRIMSON to the bottom third of the pumpkin and Medium Green to the upper left areas. Establish grooves in the stem with Dark & Very Dark Values. Highlight should be strong in the top three sections.

APPLE - Apply an accent of Green through the apple by using a mop brush to pull the paint and develop streaks. Highlight the front upper portion. Define and detail the stem.

GREEN APPLE -

Accent the lower side of each grape with the Pumpkin Medium to Light Values. Add a little red to mix if it appears too intense. Re-establish the shape of your grapes. Add high shines, keeping in mind that these grapes are farthest from the light source.

GOURDS - Establish the dimple for both gourds. Add a stem to Gourd #1.

PURPLE GRAPES -

Check to see if the color of your grapes is too brown. If they are, add an accent of ALIZARIN CRIMSON to bring back some color. Place Accent of Medium Green to left of each grape.

AUTUMN HARVEST PLATE continued

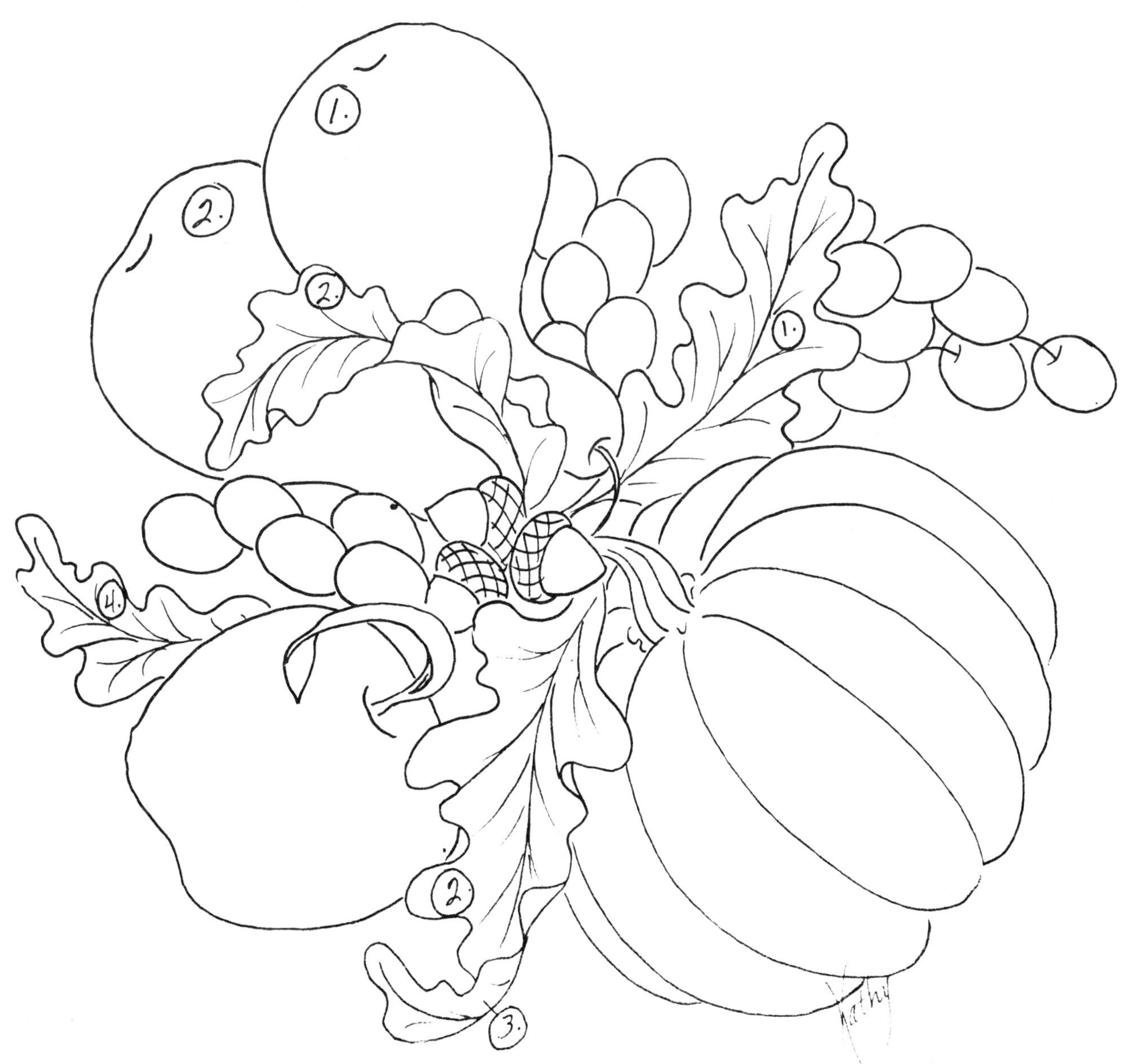

SECOND STAGE continued

ACORNS -   Crosshatch the caps with BURNT UMBER.

ALL LEAVES -

Examine each ripple to make sure that it is following the correct direction. Use a liner brush and BURNT UMBER to add spots to leaves. Line in veins, first, with BURNT UMBER, than with a light value on your palette.

FINAL STAGE -

Examine your shade areas. Does the object seem round?   Build up your highlights. Where is the light coming from? Sharpen up all edges. Cast shadows are three values of BURNT UMBER.

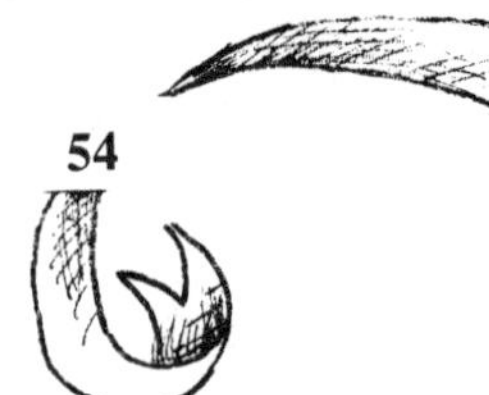

ANTIQUE CHRISTMAS BELL
ACRYLIC ON CERAMICS

SUPPLIES -

Fine Sandpaper
DecoArt "Weathered Wood"
Krylon Matte Spray #1311
Burnt Umber (any oil brand)
Thinning agent for oil paint
(Blending & Glazing Medium)

Old scruffy brushes- large & small flat
Gold Leaf - (about 2 sheets)
White glue
Baby Powder (optional)
Dust free rag (old T-shirt)

PALETTE - <u>Deco Americana Acrylics</u>

ALIZARIN CRIMSON
MILK CHOCOLATE
BLACK GREEN

BLACK PLUM
ANTIQUE GREEN

LT. BUTTERMILK
RUSSET

PREP -

1. Sand out any imperfections on the bell.
2. Base the entire bell (outside) with several coats of **ALIZARIN CRIMSON** (this paint is very transparent. Don't worry about not getting an even coverage).
3. Apply a thin coat of WEATHERED WOOD to sections #1, #4, #7 & #9 (use choppy, back-and-fourth strokes to assure small cracks). Let dry. Brush on 1 even coat of LIGHT BUTTER MILK over the WEATHERED WOOD (Be careful not to paint any overlapping coats, as it will pull off the layer below).
4. Use an old scruffy brush to paint on a thin coat of white glue over sections #2, #6 & #8. Let it set up for about 5 minutes. Apply the Gold Leaf in small pieces. Let a little of the red back ground color show through. Try to keep the edges straight (you can paint on more glue and fill in Gold Leaf in spots that didn't stick). Now, use a large scruffy brush to brush off the excess Gold Leafing.
5. Because the pattern is difficult to see over the crackling, I suggest transferring a small portion of the pattern at a time, painting that portion & then adding more pattern as you go.

DETAILED INSTRUCTIONS - LIGHT SOURCE - Middle front
RIBBON

1. Base the ribbon with 2 coats of ALIZARIN CRIMSON.
2. Shade with BLACK PLUM at overlaps and flip-float occasionaly to form ripples. Highlight with flip-floats of ALIZARIN CRIMSON + LIGHT BUTTERMILK.

LEAVES

1. Wash with 2 coats of ANTIQUE GREEN.
2. Flip-float BLACK GREEN down the center of each leaf. Also, shade to seperate leaves, deepening the shade behind the pine cone.
3. Line with BLACK GREEN for vein lines and at edge.

PINE CONE

1. Use a small flat brush. Tip into MILK CHOCOLATE. Using the chisel edge of the brush, slice the brush up-and-back to make tiny squares (like bricks).
2. Shade the left side and a little on the right side of the cone with RUSSET.
3. Highlight with LIGHT BUTTERMILK on the middle petals.

BERRIES

1. Base with 2 coats of ALIZARIN CRIMSON.
2. Shade to the left with BLACK PLUM, highlight to the right by adding WHITE to ALIZARIN CRIMSON.
3. Stems are BLACK GREEN.

ANTIQUE CHRISTMAS BELL continued

HOW TO ANTIQUE THE BELL
1. Spray the bell with 2 coats of Krylon Matte Spray.
2. Thin BURNT UMBER oil paint with Blending and Glazing Medium. Brush over bell and wipe off with rag.
3. Darken the bottom of sections #1 and 7.

FINISHING
1. Follow regular finishing procedures.
2. Tie a heavy thread to inside & attach a bead to string for a clapper just short of the end of bell.

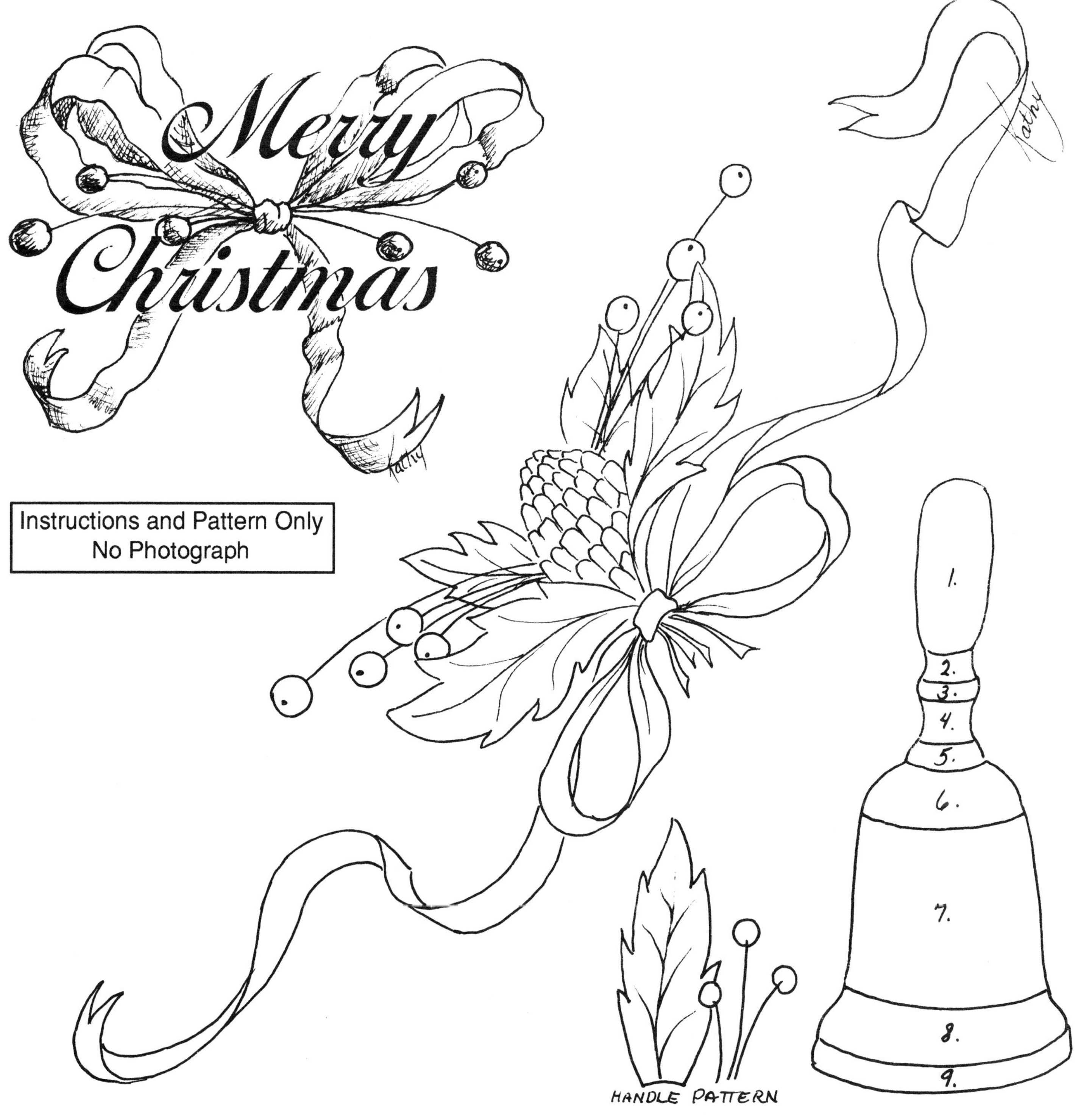

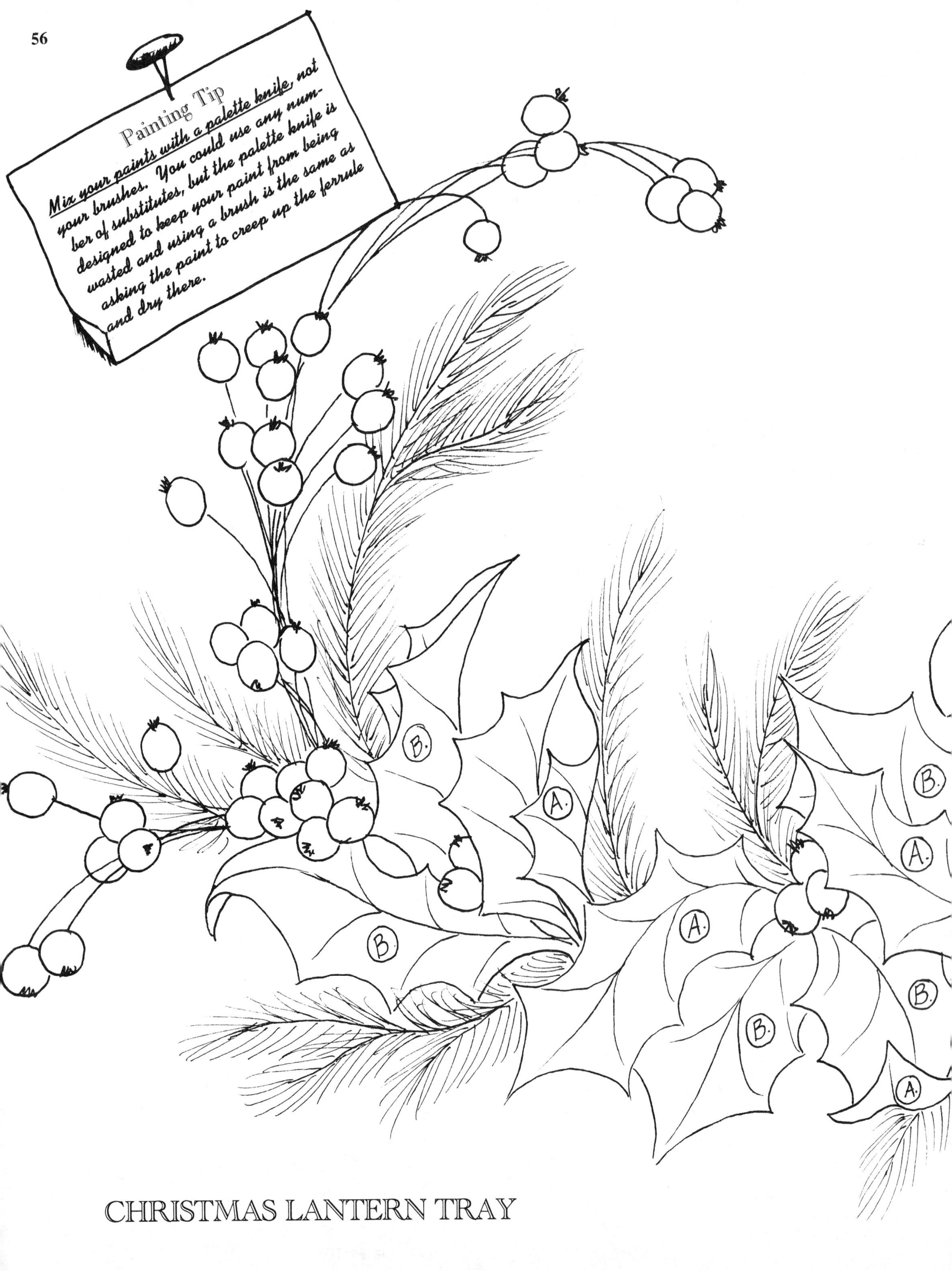

CHRISTMAS LANTERN TRAY

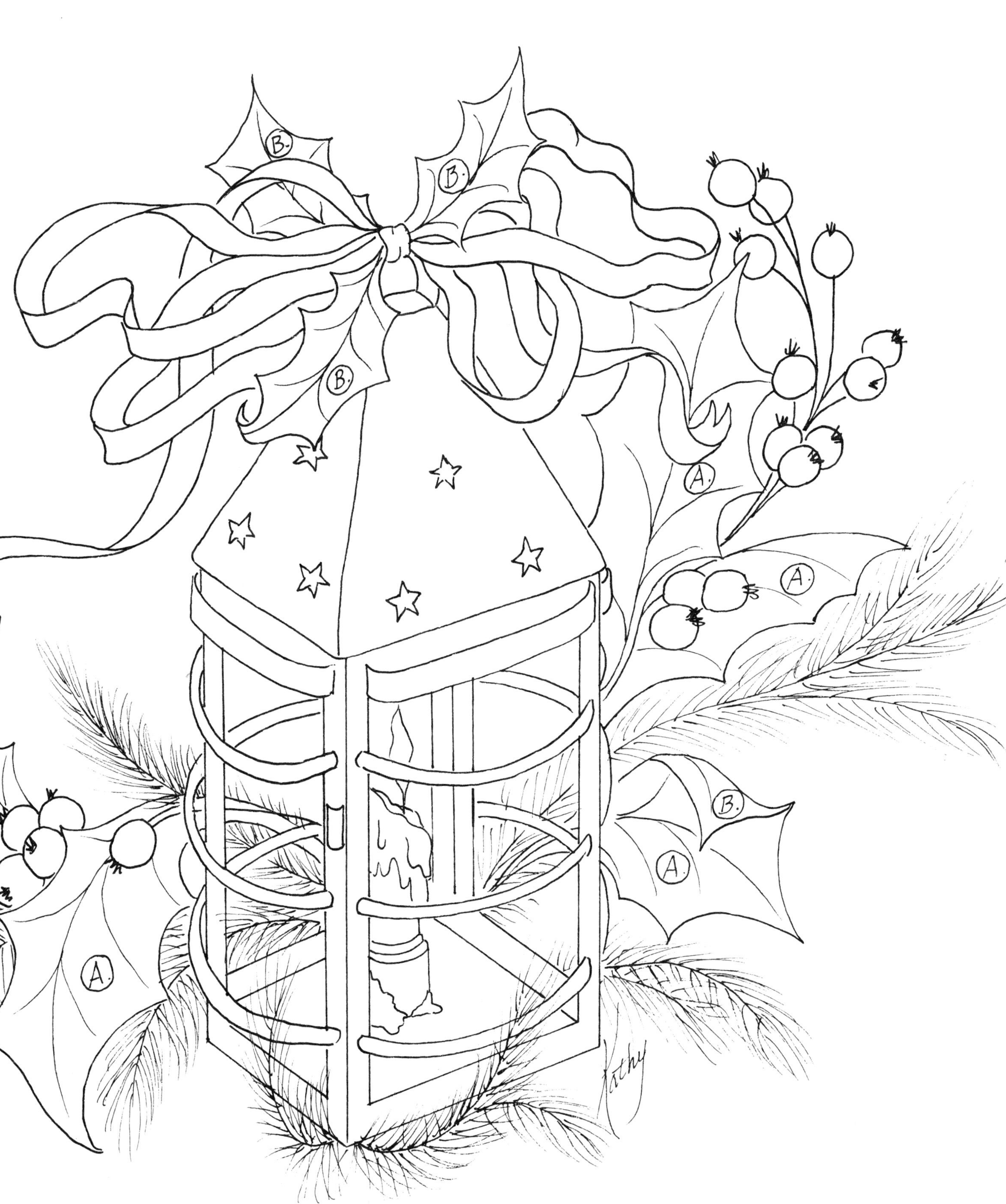

Christmas Lantern Tray
ACRYLIC

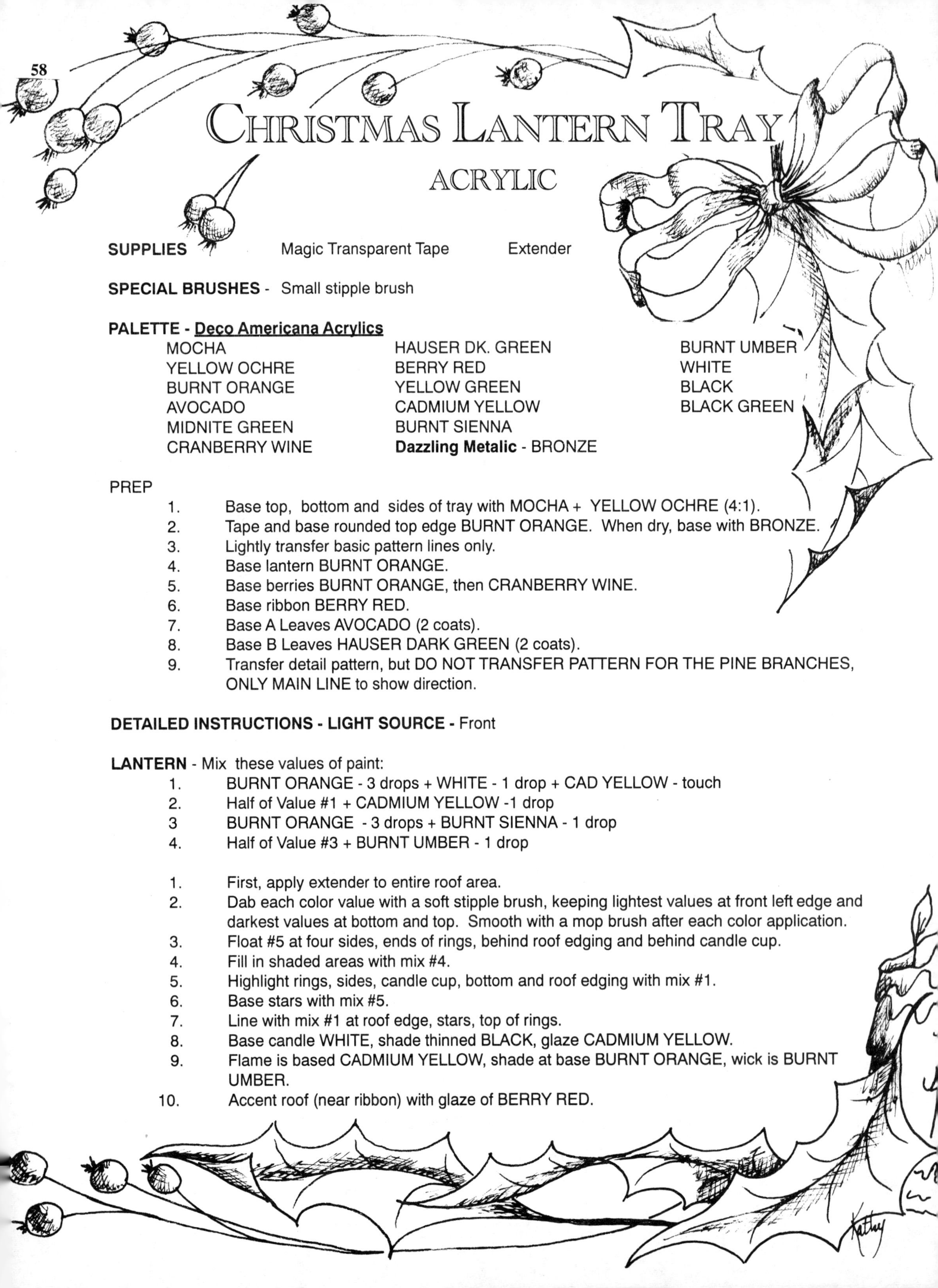

SUPPLIES   Magic Transparent Tape   Extender

SPECIAL BRUSHES - Small stipple brush

PALETTE - <u>Deco Americana Acrylics</u>

MOCHA	HAUSER DK. GREEN	BURNT UMBER
YELLOW OCHRE	BERRY RED	WHITE
BURNT ORANGE	YELLOW GREEN	BLACK
AVOCADO	CADMIUM YELLOW	BLACK GREEN
MIDNITE GREEN	BURNT SIENNA	
CRANBERRY WINE	**Dazzling Metalic** - BRONZE	

PREP

1. Base top, bottom and sides of tray with MOCHA + YELLOW OCHRE (4:1).
2. Tape and base rounded top edge BURNT ORANGE. When dry, base with BRONZE.
3. Lightly transfer basic pattern lines only.
4. Base lantern BURNT ORANGE.
5. Base berries BURNT ORANGE, then CRANBERRY WINE.
6. Base ribbon BERRY RED.
7. Base A Leaves AVOCADO (2 coats).
8. Base B Leaves HAUSER DARK GREEN (2 coats).
9. Transfer detail pattern, but DO NOT TRANSFER PATTERN FOR THE PINE BRANCHES, ONLY MAIN LINE to show direction.

DETAILED INSTRUCTIONS - LIGHT SOURCE - Front

LANTERN - Mix these values of paint:

1. BURNT ORANGE - 3 drops + WHITE - 1 drop + CAD YELLOW - touch
2. Half of Value #1 + CADMIUM YELLOW -1 drop
3. BURNT ORANGE - 3 drops + BURNT SIENNA - 1 drop
4. Half of Value #3 + BURNT UMBER - 1 drop

1. First, apply extender to entire roof area.
2. Dab each color value with a soft stipple brush, keeping lightest values at front left edge and darkest values at bottom and top. Smooth with a mop brush after each color application.
3. Float #5 at four sides, ends of rings, behind roof edging and behind candle cup.
4. Fill in shaded areas with mix #4.
5. Highlight rings, sides, candle cup, bottom and roof edging with mix #1.
6. Base stars with mix #5.
7. Line with mix #1 at roof edge, stars, top of rings.
8. Base candle WHITE, shade thinned BLACK, glaze CADMIUM YELLOW.
9. Flame is based CADMIUM YELLOW, shade at base BURNT ORANGE, wick is BURNT UMBER.
10. Accent roof (near ribbon) with glaze of BERRY RED.

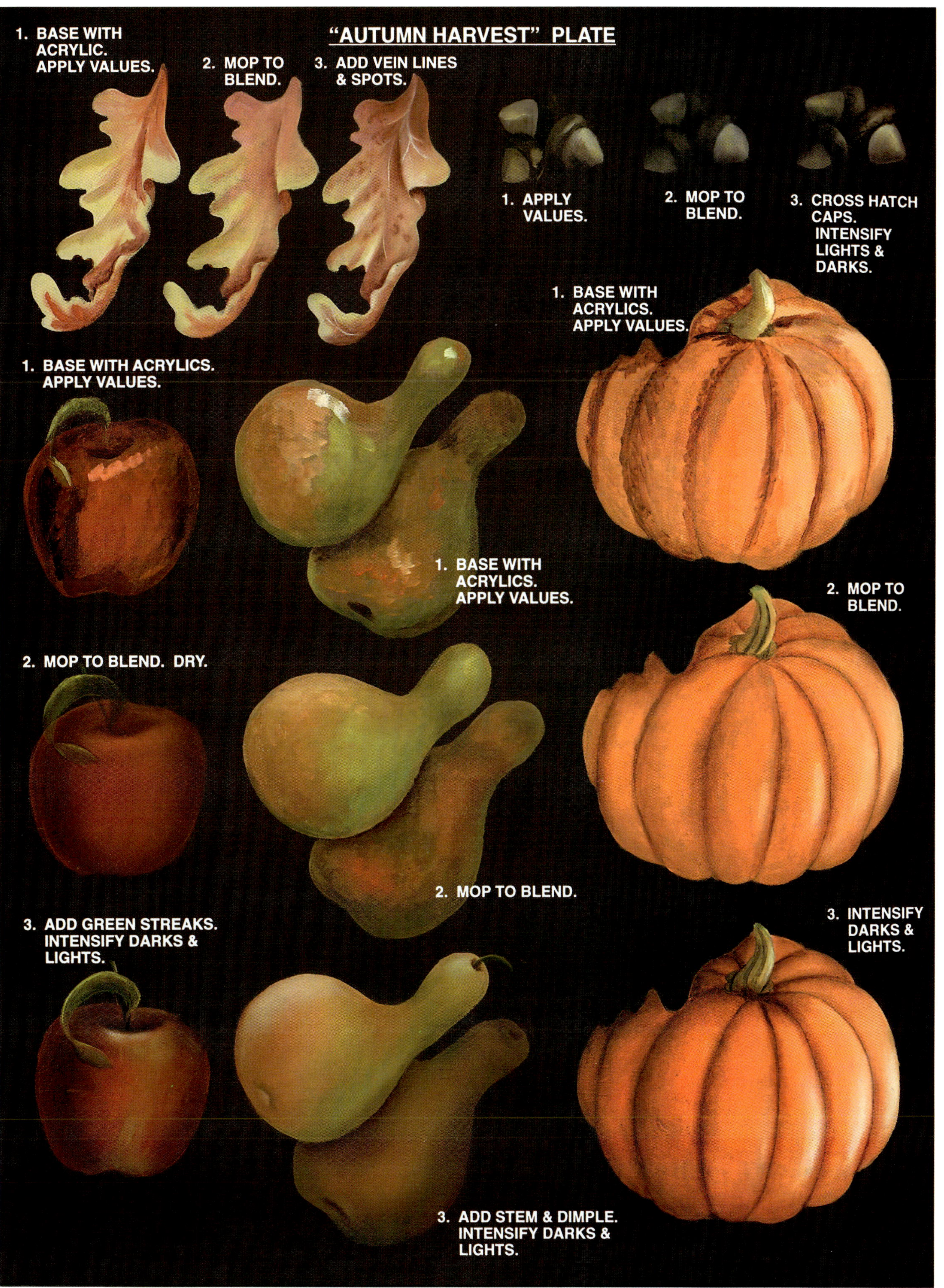
"AUTUMN HARVEST" PLATE
1. BASE WITH ACRYLIC. APPLY VALUES.
2. MOP TO BLEND.
3. ADD VEIN LINES & SPOTS.
1. APPLY VALUES.
2. MOP TO BLEND.
3. CROSS HATCH CAPS. INTENSIFY LIGHTS & DARKS.
1. BASE WITH ACRYLICS. APPLY VALUES.
1. BASE WITH ACRYLICS. APPLY VALUES.
1. BASE WITH ACRYLICS. APPLY VALUES.
2. MOP TO BLEND.
2. MOP TO BLEND. DRY.
2. MOP TO BLEND.
3. INTENSIFY DARKS & LIGHTS.
3. ADD GREEN STREAKS. INTENSIFY DARKS & LIGHTS.
3. ADD STEM & DIMPLE. INTENSIFY DARKS & LIGHTS.

HOW TO PAINT GRAPES IN OIL & ACRYLIC

GRAPES ARE DIFFERENT SHAPES DEPENDING ON WHERE THEY REST IN THE BUNCH.

OIL

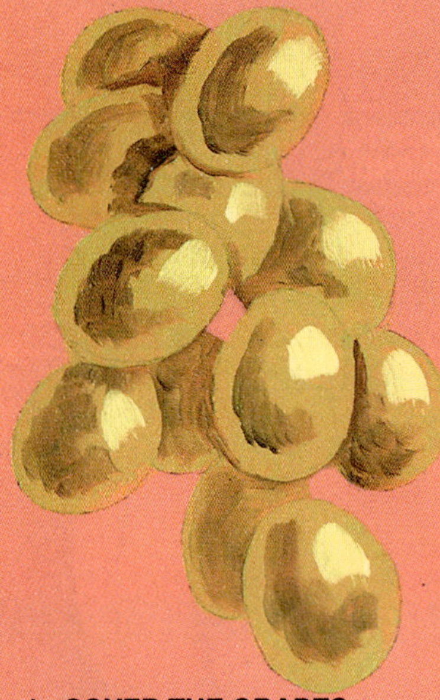 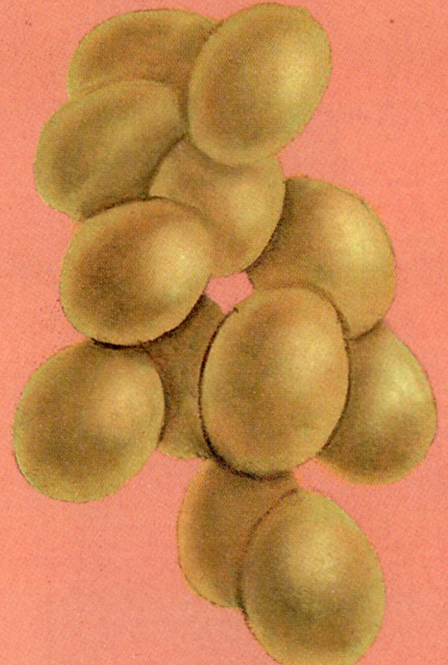 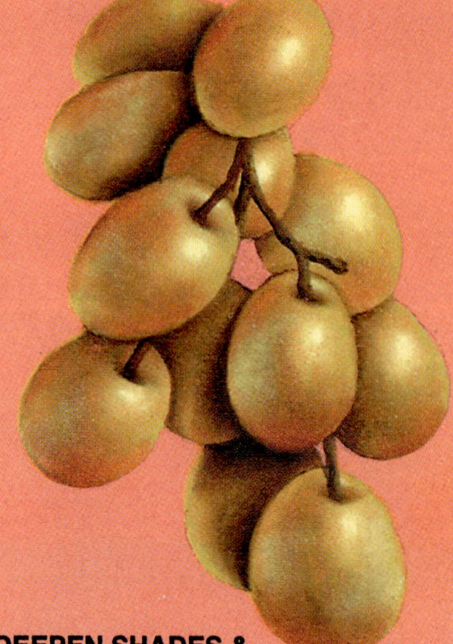

1. COVER THE GRAPES
   W/BASE MIX
   (LET A LITTLE
   BACKGROUND
   COLOR SHOW THOUGH).

2. ADD SHADING IN A
   CRESCENT SHAPE
   TO LIFT AND OVERLAP.

3. ADD LIGHT VALUE TO
   UPPER RIGHT
   AREA OF EACH GRAPE.

4. MOP TO BLEND.

5. LET DRY OR MIST
   WITH KRYLON

6. DEEPEN SHADES &
   DEFINE EDGES.

7. BUILD UP HIGHLIGHT SPOTS.

8. APPLY ACCENT COLORS OF
   SURROUNDING ITEMS.

9. ADD STEMS USING GREEN
   MIXES & BURNT UMBER.

ACRYLICS

3. FLIP - FLOAT SHADE IN A CRESCENT
   SHAPE. MOP TO BLEND.

6. APPLY ACCENT COLORS OF
   SURROUNDING ITEMS.

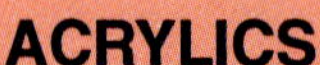

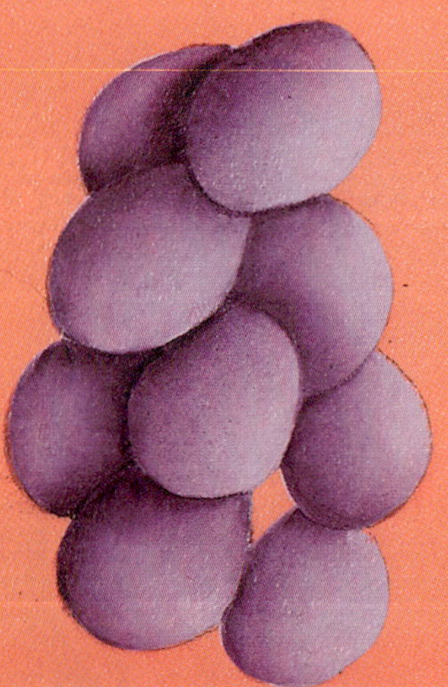 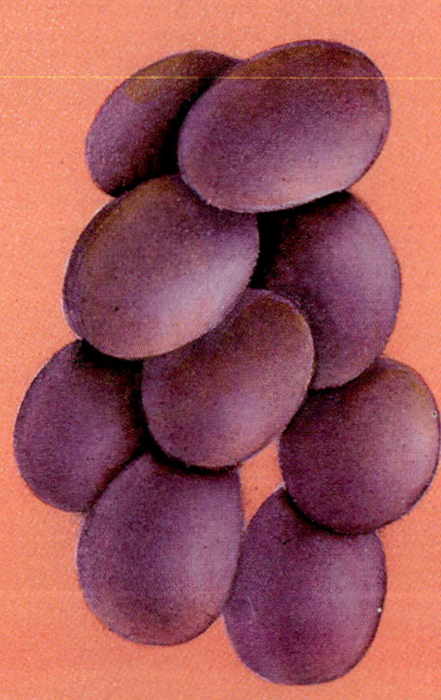 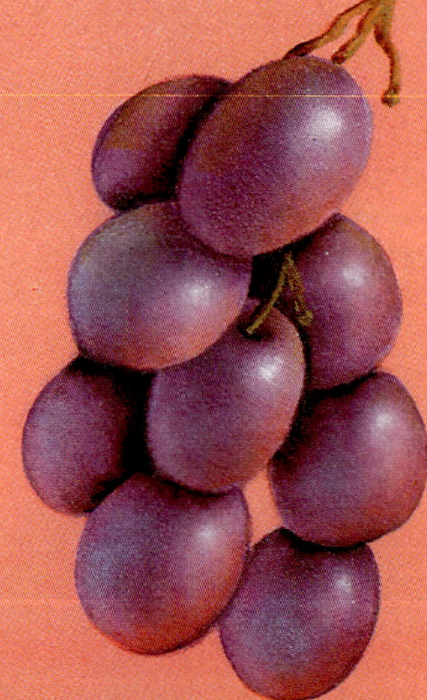

1. APPLY BASE COLOR.

2. SHADE AT OVERLAPS &
   AT LEFT SIDE.

4. DEEPEN SHADE &
   SHARPEN EDGES.

5. SHADE AT EDGE ON RIGHT SIDE.

7. BUILD UP HIGHLIGHTS
   WITH BASE COLOR & WHITE,
   THEN WHITE ONLY.

8. ADD DIMPLE & STEMS.

CHRISTMAS LANTERN TRAY continued

BERRIES
1. Shade CRANBERRY WINE + BLACK (5:1) at the farthest side from light of candle on each berry.
2. Float BLACK to separate each berry and where leaves overlap.
3. Highlight BERRY RED + WHITE (4:1) at side nearest light. Repeat highlight with WHITE when dry. Place highlight (window) nearest light on each berry and a highlight dot.
4. Glaze over highlighted areas of berries with CADMIUM YELLOW.
5. Ends of each berry are BLACK.
6. Stems and branches are BLACK + BURNT SIENNA (1:1).

HOLLY LEAVES
1. Shade with a flip-float of BLACK GREEN down center vein area and side vein line areas.
2. Line over shading on all vein lines with YELLOW GREEN + CADMIUM YELLOW (2:1).
3. Shade between vein lines with BLACK GREEN.
4. Highlight in middle of scallops with CADMIUM YELLOW then WHITE (toward light). Add highlight to vein lines in some places.
5. Accent in some places BURNT ORANGE and BERRY RED.
6. Line the edges to make points sharp on each leaf.
7. Shade between and behind leaves with thinned MIDNITE GREEN.

RIBBON
1. Shade at overlaps and flips with BERRY RED and BLACK (3:1).
2. Highlight with BERRY RED + WHITE (3.1) where light would reflect. Use a flip-float. Repeat with WHITE (two reflection lines where light is brightest).

PINE BRANCHES
1. Using a 10/0 liner, establish center line with BLACK GREEN (pull all strokes from this line, out).
2. Stroke several pine needles of - BLACK GREEN, AVOCADO, AVOCADO + WHITE (only a few towards light).
3. With a thinned coat of WHITE, cover the entire glass area, then streak with WHITE (for reflections).

FINISHING - Follow regular finishing procedures.

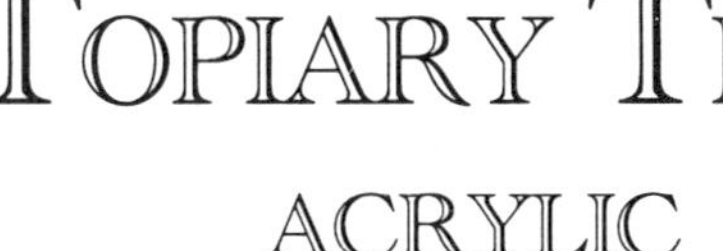

TOPIARY TREE
ACRYLIC

SUPPLIES
Old toothbrush or fan brush   Extenter

PALETTE - <u>Deco Americana Acrylics</u>
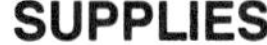

BUTTERMILK	ANTIQUE GOLD DEEP	SHALE GREEN
COUNTRY BLUE	SABLE BROWN	PEACHES & CREAM
JADE GREEN	BLACK PLUM	BURNT UMBER
ANTIQUE WHITE	PLANTATION PINE	ANTIQUE ROSE
PINEAPPLE	ANTIQUE GREEN	WHITE
ROYAL PURPLE	RUSSET	MIDNITE GREEN
BLACK GREEN	BURNT ORANGE	RED IRON OXIDE
ASPHALTUM		

TOPIARY TREE continued
PREP -
1. Apply a heavy wash of 4 parts BUTTERMILK, I part SABLE BROWN to both front and back of wood.
2. Straight side of routed edge is based RUSSET.
3. Curved side of routed edge is based RED IRON OXIDE.
4. Transfer lightly basic pattern lines only.
5. "Splatter" BURNT ORANGE over front surface.
6. Apply these base colors as follows......
   PEARS - Wash with 2 coats PINEAPPLE
   APPLES - Wash with 2 coats mix of PEACHES & CREAM + RUSSET
   RIBBON , ROSES and BUDS - Wash with 2 coats BUTTERMILK.
   GRAPES - (purple and green) Wash with I coat of ANTIQUE GOLD DEEP.
   PLUMS - Wash with 2 thin coats of RUSSET.
   DAISIES - Base with 2 coats of WHITE.
   TRUNK - Base with 2 coats ANTIQUE WHITE.
   CLAY POT - Base 2 coats of mix of RED IRON OXIDE + WHITE.
   LEAVES #I - Wash with I coat of SHALE GREEN.
   LEAVES #2- Wash with I coat of JADE GREEN.
7. Transfer detail pattern lines lightly.

DETAILED INSTRUCTIONS - LIGHT SOURCE - Upper Right

PEARS
1. Shade with ANTIQUE GOLD DEEP.
2. Deepen shade with ANTIQUE GREEN, then PLANTATION PINE in the deepest areas.
3. Cast shadows are BLACK GREEN.
4. Highlights are first ANTIQUE GOLD DEEP + WHITE, sparkle shine is WHITE only.
5. Accent color on left edge.
6. Reflective light on left edge is MIDNITE GREEN + ANTIQUE GOLD DEEP + WHITE
7. Accent color is BURNT ORANGE + extender.

APPLES
1. Apply ANTIQUE GOLD DEEP to some areas for contrast.
2. Apply ANTIQUE ROSE iike a wash over most of the apple (except the green areas).
3. Shade with RUSSET at left, under leaves & flip-float at bottom end of apple to create curves.
4. Deepen the shade by adding a little MIDNITE GREEN to RUSSET.
5. Highlight with ANTIQUE ROSE + •RUSSET + WHITE, sparkle shine with WHITE only.
6. Blossom ends are lined with RUSSET + BLACK PLUM.
7. Reflective light on the edge of the apple on the left is ANTIQUE ROSE + extender.

PLUMS
1. Apply a wash of ROYAL PURPLE.
2. Shade with BLACK PLUM at edge and at left edge.
3. Highlight with ROYAL PURPLE + WHITE, sparkle shine is WHITE.
4. Yeast mold is stippled WHITE + COUNTRY BLUE.
5. Accent with ANTIQUE ROSE + extender.

ROSES & BUDS
1. Accent first with I/2 ANTIQUE GOLD DEEP + PINEAPPLE to the base of each open petal.
2. Apply a flip-float of ANTIQUE ROSE to make ripples in some petals.
3. Shade at the base and overlaps of each petal with RUSSET.
4. Shade with RUSSET + MIDNITE GREEN in the deepest shaded areas only.
5. Highlight with WHITE (mainly on the right side of the roses).

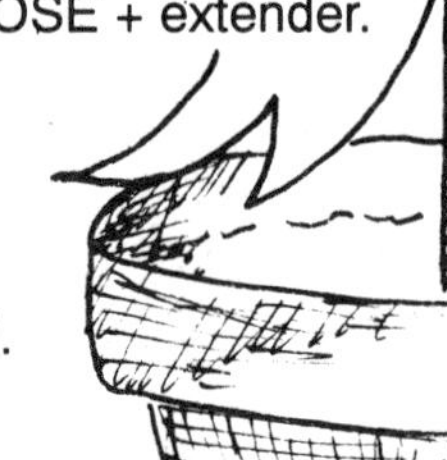

DAISIES

  I. Base centers 1/2 ANTIQUE GOLD DEEP + 1/2 PINEAPPLE + •BURNT UMBER, shade and dots RUSSET.
  2. Shade with RED IRON OXIDE between each petal.
  3. Shade again with RUSSET in deepest areas.
  4. Re-establish WHITE for the highlight.
  5. Accent with ANTIQUE GOLD DEEP and ROYAL PURPLE + extender.

TRUNK

  I. Shade and line with BURNT UMBER.
  2. Deepen shade near bow and cast shadow with ASPHALTUM.
  3. Accent with RED IRON OXIDE + extender.

GREEN GRAPES

  I. Shade with PLANTATION PINE behind each grape.
  2. Shade left side of each grape with ANTIQUE GREEN + •RUSSET.
  3. Deepen shade for cast shadows with MIDNITE GREEN.
  4. Highlight is ANTIQUE GOLD DEEP + WHITE, sparkle shine is WHITE.
  5. Accent color is ROYAL PURPLE on the right side and ANTIQUE ROSE on the left.
  6. Reflective light on the left side is ANTIQUE GOLD DEEP + WHITE + extender.
  7. Yeast mold is stippled with COUNTRY BLUE.
  8. Stems are Rose Values.

PURPLE GRAPES

  I. Shade with ROYAL PURPLE + •BLACK PLUM to the left side of each grape.
  2. Deepen shade at overlaps with BLACK PLUM only.
  3. Highlight with ROYAL PURPLE + WHITE, sparkle shine is WHITE.
  4. Reflective light on left is ANTIQUE GOLD DEEP + extender and ANTIQUE ROSE + extender on right.
  5. Yeast mold is stippled COUNTRY BLUE.

RIBBON & BOW

  I. Shade at overlaps & flip-floats with RED IRON OXIDE.
  2.   Shade across the entire top part of the ribbon & bow with RED IRON OXIDE.
  3. Deepen at overlaps with RUSSET.
  4. Add •BLACK PLUM to RUSSET for deepest shades.
  5. Re-establish highlights with WHITE.
  6. Reflective light ROYAL PURPLE and ANTIQUE GOLD DEEP on left side ANTIQUE ROSE on right.

CLAY POT

  I. Shade with RED IRON OXIDE.
  2. Deepen with RUSSET.
  3. Highlight with WHITE + RED IRON OXIDE.
  4. Dirt is BURNT UMBER.

ALL LEAVES

  I. Shade with PLANTATION PINE down middle, at the base and at overlaps of each leaf.
  2. Shade at some side vein lines with same.
  3. Deepen shade at base & overlaps with BLACK GREEN.
  4. Vein lines PLANTATION PINE on shade areas, JADE GREEN on highlighted areas (apply with broken lines and fade out in shadows).
  5. Highlight with base color + WHITE, sparkle shine is WHITE.
  6. Accent color is RED IRON OXIDE + extender.
  7. Sharpen edges of leaves, line MIDNITE GREEN in some areas. Add RED IRON OXIDE to rose leaves edges only.

FINISHING - Follow regular finishing procedures.

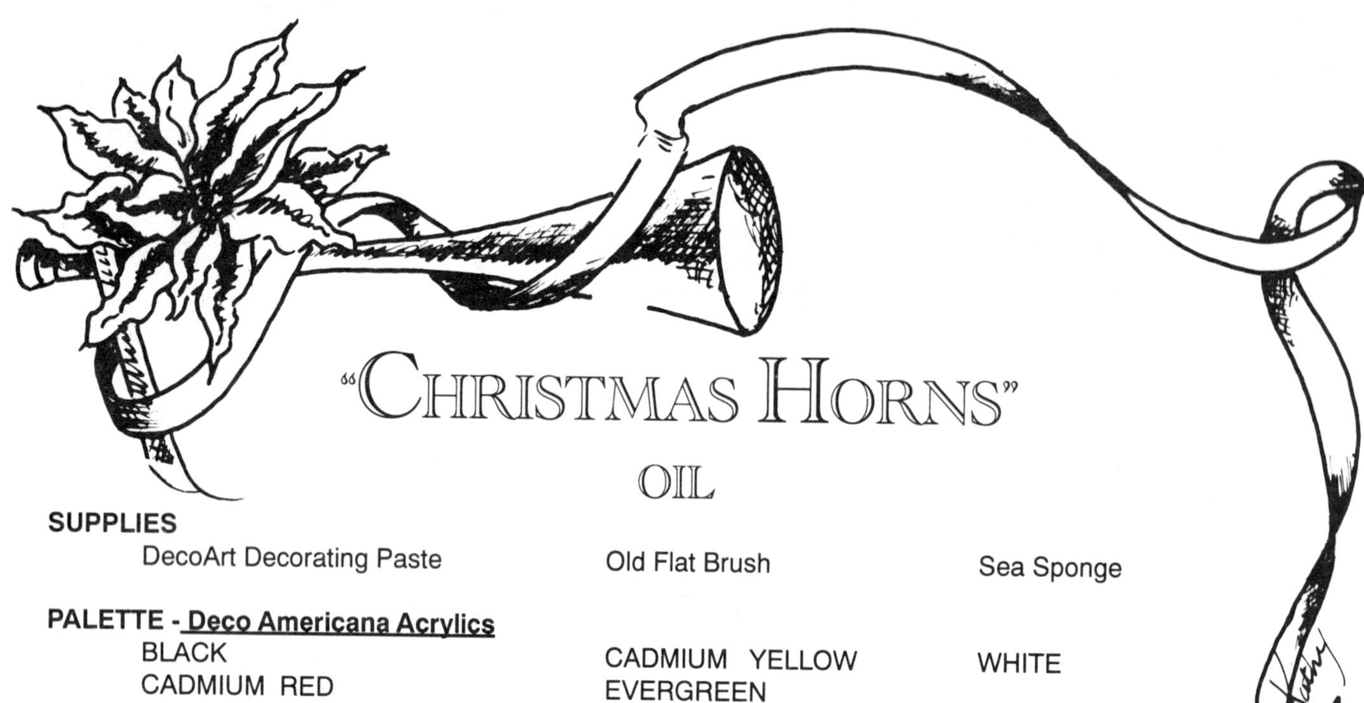

"CHRISTMAS HORNS"
OIL

SUPPLIES

DecoArt Decorating Paste   Old Flat Brush   Sea Sponge

PALETTE - <u>Deco Americana Acrylics</u>

BLACK	CADMIUM YELLOW	WHITE
CADMIUM RED	EVERGREEN	

Winsor & Newton Oils

TITANIUM WHITE	ALIZARIN CRIMSON	NAPLES YELLOW
CADMIUM YELLOW	COBALT BLUE	BURNT UMBER
CADMIUM RED	BLACK	RAW SIENNA

PREP

1. With an old flat brush, liberally apply the Decorating Paste over all 4 sides of the box. Now, with a sea sponge, pat gingerly over the pasted areas to form texture. Set aside to dry for 4 hours. When dry, paint this area BLACK.
2. Base all parts of the box and lid BLACK except the routed edges.
3. Base the top side of the base piece and the front edge of both the box and the lid EVERGREEN. Base the routed edges on both the box & the lid CADMIUM RED.
4. Transfer the basic pattern, lightly. Do not transfer the pointsettia centers at this time.
5. Base these opaque: The horns - Acrylic CADMIUM YELLOW, the pointsettia petals Acrylic CADMIUM RED and the ribbon Acrylic WHITE.

DETAILED INSTRUCTIONS - LIGHT SOURCE - Right
POINTSETTIA PETALS

Medium Value -	5 parts CADMIUM RED + 1 part ALIZARIN CRIMSON
Light Value -	4 parts Medium Value + 1 part WHITE
Highlight Value -	WHITE + •Light Value
Dark Value -	1 part Medium Value + 1 part ALIZARIN CRIMSON + •BLACK
Very Dark Value -	ALIZARIN CRIMSON + •BLACK
Accent -	CADMIUM YELLOW

Because the light is coming from the right, use lighter values in the petals to the right and darker values to form the petals on the left. Very Dark Value is placed in the middle of each petal and mopped outward to form an area for the vein line.

POINTSETTIA CENTERS

The petal pods (casing around the berries) are Leaves Medium Value to Light Value. The berries are Pointsettia Medium Value to Dark Value. Both have highlights of CADMIUM YELLOW.

POINTSETTIA LEAVES

Medium Value -	3 parts COBALT BLUE + 2 parts CADMIUM YELLOW + 1 part WHITE
Light Value -	1 part Medium Value + 1 part WHITE
Highlight Value -	WHITE + •Light Value
Dark Value -	2 parts COBALT BLUE + 2 parts CADMIUM YELLOW
Very Dark Value -	Dark Value + •BLACK

The leaves are veined with Leaves Light Value, but softly mopped out as they go into the shadows.

CHRISTMAS HORNS continued

HORNS -

Medium Value -	2 parts CADMIUM YELLOW + 1 part BURNT SIENNA
Light Value -	1 part Medium Value + 1 part WHITE
Hightlight Value -	WHITE + • Light Value
Dark Value -	1 part Medium Value + 1 part BURNT SIENNA
Very Dark Value -	1 part BURNT UMBER + 1 part BURNT SIENNA
Reflection -	Pointsettia Medium Value
Reflection -	Leaves Medium Value

Place values in their proper order. Gently mop the values together, but don't blend out the value sections. Light and shadows reflected on this long gold metal will cast long sections of colors. As it approaches the bowl of the horn, the colors spread out and are softer and more blended.

RIBBON

Medium Value -	2 parts WHITE + 1 part BLACK + 1 part Leaves Medium Value
Light Value -	1 part Medium Value + 1 part WHITE
Highlight Value -	WHITE + •Light Value
Dark Value -	2 parts WHITE + 1 part Medium Value
Very Dark Value -	1 part Dark Value + 1 part BLACK + 1 part Leaves Medium Value
Accent -	Pointsettia Petals Medium Value
Accent -	Leaves Medium Value

After placing values in appropriate areas, mop to blend. Spray with Krylon Matte when finished. When dry, blend accents in areas that would cast reflections onto the ribbon and redefine the highlight areas with WHITE.

FINISHING

1.   Follow regular finishing procedures.
2. Cover the bottom of the inside with a matching velvet.
3. Reattach the hinges.

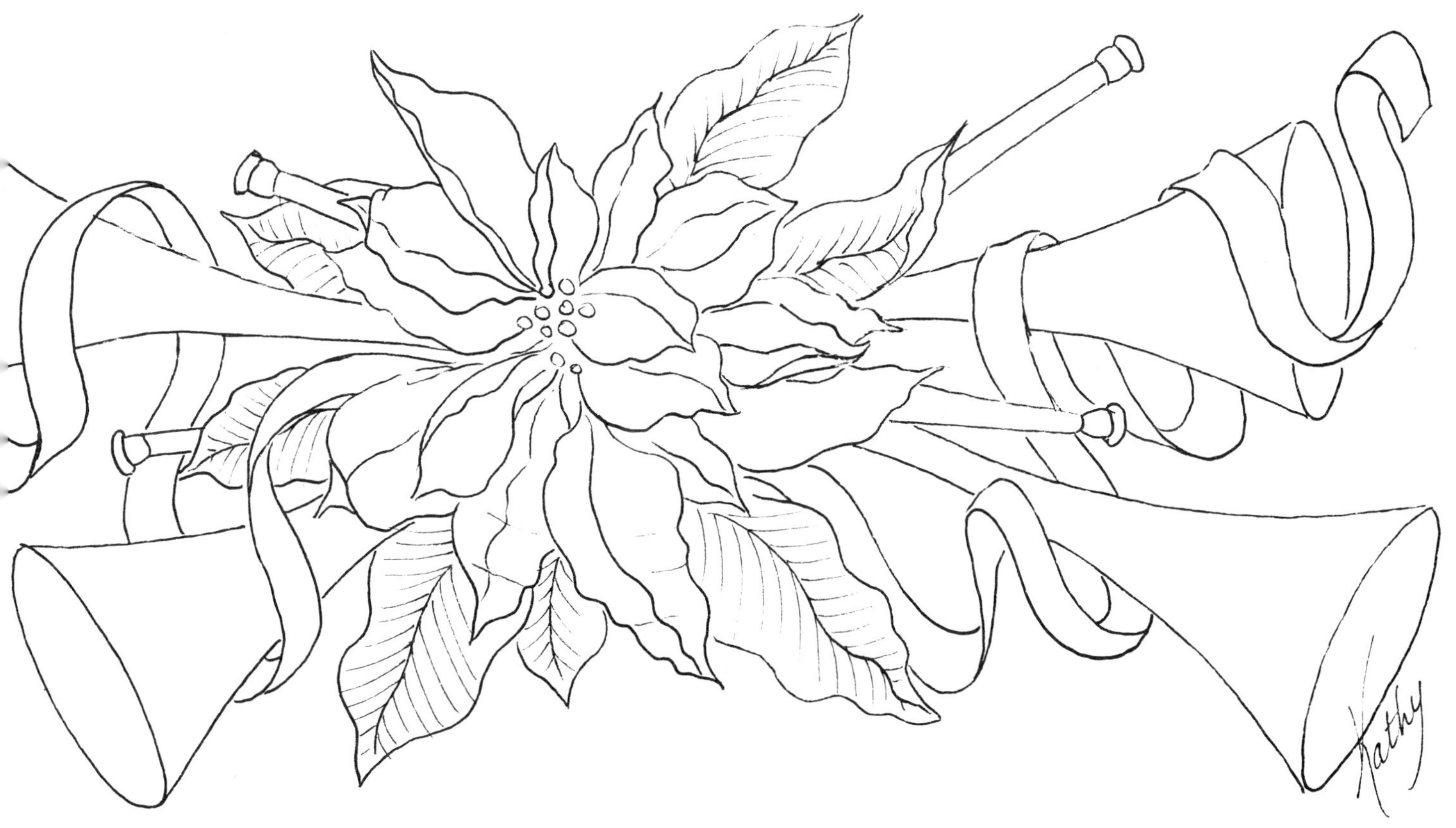

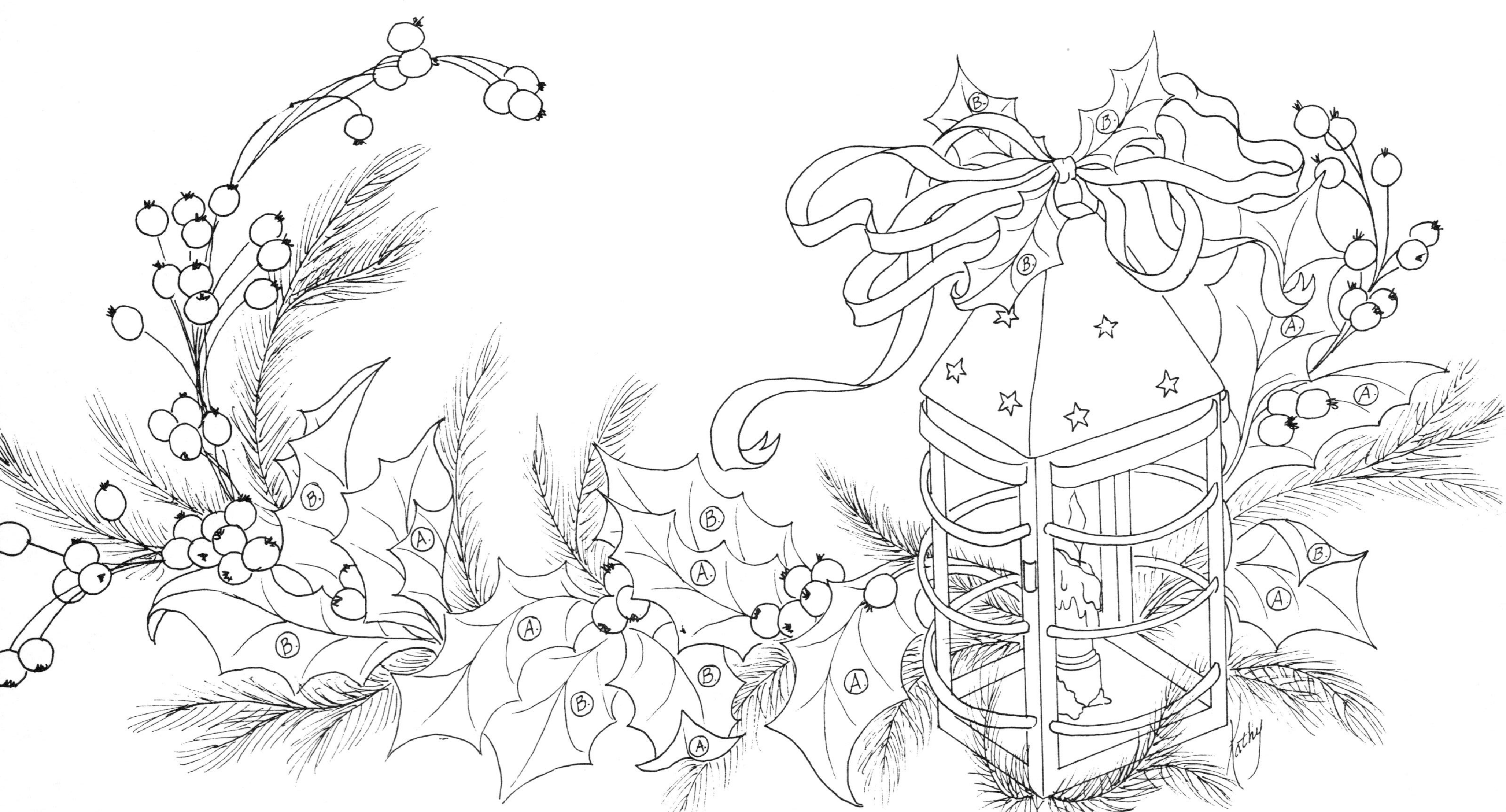

CHRISTMAS LANTERN TRAY

—— ACRYLIC BOOKS ——

Vol.	Title / Author	#	Price
ol. 19	"Gift of Painting" by Susan Scheewe	230	$9.50___
ol. 1	"Painting It's Our Bag" by Bev Hink/Susan Scheewe	193	$9.50___
ol. 4	"Keepsake Sampler" by Susan & Camille Scheewe	200	$9.50___
ol. 1	"Keepsakes For The Holidays" by C. Stempel & S. Scheewe	286	$9.50___
ol. 1	"Bumbleberries" by Connie Aloise ....*NEW*	412	$9.50___
ol. 2	'Country Heartworks 2" by Reed Baxter	365	$9.50___
ol. 3	"Country Heartworks 3" by Reed Baxter	402	$9.50___
ol. 1	"Plain Folk" by Ginger Barlage	389	$9.50___
ol. 1	"Kids And Water" by Joyce Benner	234	$9.50___
ol. 2	"The Flower Market" by Joyce Benner	319	$9.50___
ol. 3	"Country Fixin's - For All Seasons" by Rhonda Caldwell	332	$9.50___
ol. 1	"Country Celebration" by Tammy Christensen	378	$9.50___
ol. 1	"A Painters Garden" by Jane Dillon	354	$9.50___
ol. 2	"A Painter's Garden 2" by Jane Dillon ....*NEW*	411	$9.50___
ol. 1	"Santas and Sams" by Bobi Dolara	258	$9.50___
ol. 2	"Vintage Peace" by Bobi Dolara	270	$9.50___
ol. 2	"Floral Designs 2" by Carol Empet	338	$9.50___
ol. 3	"Floral Portraits" by Carol Empet	358	$9.50___
ol. 1	"Angels Are Near" by Carol Freeman & Brenda Turley	375	$9.50___
ol. 1	"Briar Patch" by Sandy Fochler	380	$9.50___
ol. 2	"Briar Patch #2" by Sandy Fochler ....*NEW*	424	$9.50___
ol. 1	"Romantically Tole Bauernmalerei" by Sherry Gall	311	$9.50___
ol. 2	"Deck The Halls Bauernmalerei" by Sherry Gall	391	$9.50___
ol. 1	"Olde Thyme Folk Art" by Teresa Gregory	390	$9.50___
ol. 2	"Country Thyme" by Teresa Gregory	406	$9.50___
ol. 1	'Windchimes, Weathervanes & Welcomes" by Vickie Higley	386	$9.50___
ol. 1	"Holiday Gathering" by Angie Hupp	267	$9.50___
ol. 3	"Heavenly Gathering" by Angie Hupp	320	$9.50___
ol. 1	"Happy Heart, Happy Home" by Cathy Jones	241	$9.50___
ol. 1	"Dandelions" by Carla Kern ....*NEW*	416	$9.50___
ol. 1	"Pickets & Pastimes" by Marie & Jim King	329	$9.50___
ol. 3	"Pickets & Pastimes 3, Feathered Inns" by M. & J. King	385	$9.50___
ol. 1	"For Me & My House" by Myrna King	370	$9.50___
ol. 1	"Huckleberry Horse" by Hanna Long	269	$9.50___
ol. 2	"Love Lives Here" by Mary Lynn Lewis	185	$9.50___
ol. 3	"Love Lives Here" by Mary Lynn Lewis	195	$6.50___
ol. 1	"Everything Under The Moon" by Jackie Ludwig ....*NEW*	421	$9.50___
ol. 1	"Second Nature" by Kathy McPherson ....*NEW*	427	$9.50___
ol. 2	"Special Welcomes" by Corinne Miller	298	$9.50___
ol. 3	"Special Welcomes #3, Crazy About Crafting" by Corinne Miller	309	$9.50___
ol. 5	"Special Welcomes #5 All Wrapped Up" by Corinne Miller	333	$9.50___
ol. 6	"Special Welcomes #6 Crop Keepers" by Corinne Miller	347	$9.50___
ol. 1	"Fruit & Flower Fantasies" by Joyce Morrison	277	$9.50___
ol. 2	"Fruit & Flower Fantasies 2" by Joyce Morrison	382	$9.50___
ol. 1	"Whimsical Critters" by Lori Ohlson	228	$7.50___
ol. 2	"Sunflower Farm" by Lori Ohlson	326	$9.50___
ol. 1	"Friends Forevermore" by Karen Ortman ....*NEW*	434	$9.50___
ol. 1	"Holiday Medley" by Nina Owens	265	$9.50___
ol. 2	"Another Holiday Medley" by Nina Owens	296	$9.50___
ol. 1	"Oh Those Little Rascals" by Diane Permenter	247	$9.50___
ol. 1	"Tailfeathers" by Gisele Pope & Carla Kern ....*NEW*	417	$9.50___
ol. 8	"Now & Then" by La Rae Parry ....*NEW*	428	$9.50___
ol. 1	"Between The Vines" by Jamie Mills Price	400	$9.50___
ol. 2	"Between The Vines 2" by Jamie Mills Price ....*NEW*	419	$9.50___
ol. 1	"Forever In My Heart" by Diane Richards.....AC/Fabric	188	$6.50___
ol. 2	"Memories In My Heart" by Diane Richards.....AC/Fabric	189	$6.50___
ol. 3	"Forever In My Heart II" by Diane Richards.....AC/Fabric	205	$9.50___
Vol. 6	"Angels In My Stocking" by Diane Richards	254	$9.50___
Vol. 7	"Nostalgic Dreams" by Diane Richards	273	$9.50___
Vol. 8	"Angel Kisses" by Diane Richards	346	$9.50___
Vol. 1	"Country Classics" by Karen Rideout ....*NEW*	413	$9.50___
Vol. 1	"Country Fun For Chistmas" by Tina Rodrigues	367	$9.50___
Vol. 2	"Country Fun 2" by Tina Rodrigues	383	$9.50___
Vol. 3	"Country At Heart" by Tina Rodrigues	401	$9.50___
Vol. 4	"Country At Heart 4" by Tina Rodrigues	410	$9.50___
Vol. 1	"Kracker Jack Kritters" by Kathie Rueger	405	$9.50___
Vol. 1	"Schoolhouse Treasures" by Cathy Schmidt	408	$9.50___
Vol. 2	"Schoolhouse Treasures" by Cathy Schmidt ....*NEW*	433	$9.50___
Vol. 1	"Holiday Hangarounds" by Marsha Sellers	327	$9.50___
Vol. 1	"Huckleberry Friends" by Cheryl Seslar	393	$9.50___
Vol. 2	"Huckleberry Friends 2" by Cheryl Seslar	403	$9.50___
Vol. 3	"Huckleberry Friends 3" by Cheryl Seslar ....*NEW*	431	$9.50___
Vol. 1	"Creations In Canvas...and More" by Carol Spooner	256	$9.50___
Vol. 1	"Gran's Garden" by Ros Stallcup	295	$9.50___
Vol. 2	"Another Gran's Garden" by Ros Stallcup	315	$9.50___
Vol. 3	"Gran's Garden & House" by Ros Stallcup	334	$9.50___
Vol. 4	"Gran's Garden Party" by Ros Stallcup	345	$9.50___
Vol. 5	"Gran's Treasures" by Ros Stallcup	363	$9.50___
Vol. 6	"Gran's Gifts" by Ros Stallcup	387	$9.50___
Vol. 7	"Gran's Welcome" by Ros Stallcup ....*NEW*	425	$9.50___
Vol. 8	"Gran's Marketplace" by Ros Stallcup ....*NEW*	426	$12.95___
Vol. 1	"Blackberry Hollow" by Margaret Steed	384	$9.50___
Vol. 2	"Blackberry Hollow" by Margaret Steed	407	$9.50___
Vol. 1	"Mrs. McGregors Garden" by Charleen Stempel	316	$9.50___
Vol. 1	"Christmas Greetings from the Cottage" by Chris Stokes	336	$9.50___
Vol. 1	"Christmas Visions" by Max Terry	278	$9.50___
Vol. 3	"Painting Clay Pot-pourri" by Max Terry	310	$9.50___
Vol. 4	"The Nesting Place" by Max Terry	373	$9.50___
Vol. 1	"Country Primitives" by Maxine Thomas	274	$9.50___
Vol. 2	"Country Primitives 2" by Maxine Thomas	300	$9.50___
Vol. 3	"Country Primitives 3" by Maxine Thomas	322	$9.50___
Vol. 4	"Country Primitives 4" by Maxine Thomas	350	$9.50___
Vol. 5	"Country Primitives 5" by Maxine Thomas	392	$9.50___
Vol. 6	"Country Primitives 6" by Maxine Thomas ....*NEW*	429	$9.50___
Vol. 1	"Rise & Shine" by Jolene Thompson	214	$6.50___
Vol. 2	"Garden Gate" by Jolene Thompson	250	$9.50___
Vol. 5	"Count Your Blessings" by Chris Thornton	213	$9.50___
Vol. 6	"Share Your Blessings" by Chris Thornton	226	$9.50___
Vol. 7	"Blessings" by Chris Thornton	255	$9.50___
Vol. 9	"Blessings For The Home" by Chris Thornton	275	$9.50___
Vol. 11	"Painted Blessings" by Chris Thornton	323	$9.50___
Vol. 12	"Family Blessings" by Chris Thornton	349	$9.50___
Vol. 13	"Garden Blessings" by Chris Thornton	356	$9.50___
Vol. 14	"Friendship Blessings" by Chris Thorton	371	$9.50___
Vol. 15	"Multitude of Blessings" by Chris Thornton	379	$9.50___
Vol. 16	"10th Aniversary of Blessings" by Chris Thornton ....*NEW*	404	$9.50___
Vol. 17	"Blessings For The Home & Garden" by Chris Thornton	423	$12.95___
Vol. 1	"Watermelon Wedges and Rustic Edges" by Lorinne Thurlow	342	$9.50___
Vol. 3	"Watermelon Wedges and Rustic Edges 3" by L. Thurlow	362	$9.50___
Vol. 2	"Farmer and Friends" by Lou Ann Trice	366	$9.50___
Vol. 5	"Daydreams & Sweet Shirts II" by Don & Lynn Weed	208	$9.50___
Vol. 1	"Pitter-Patter-Pigtail-Girls! A Simpler Thyme" by Stacy Gross West ..*NEW*	432	$9.50___
Vol. 1	"Connie's Favorite Old-Time Labels" by Connie Williams	335	$9.50___
Vol. 2	"Connie's Garden Seed Packets" by Connie Williams	351	$9.50___
Vol. 1	"Floral Fabrics and Watercolor" by Sally Williams	262	$9.50___
Vol. 1	"A Time For Giving" by Evelyn Wright	308	$9.50___
Vol. 1	"Heart Full Of Whimsy" by Mariellen Youngdahl ....*NEW*	420	$9.50___

NAME ______________________________________   5-20-98

ADDRESS __________________________________

CITY/STATE/ZIP ____________________________

____

PH (   ) ______________________________

VISA ______________________________________

M/C _______________________________________

EXP. DATE _________________________________

SHIPPING $ ________________________________

SHIP TO: __________________________________

****
SHIPPING & HANDLING CHARGES
Add $3.00 for the First Book for shipping and handling.
Add $1.50 per each additional book.

Please Add $4.00 for handling & postage. PER TAPES. <u>Sorry we must have a "NO REFUND - NO RETURN" policy.</u>

U.S CURRENCY

LOOK FOR US ON-LINE!
http://www.painting-books.com
e-mail us: SCHEEWEPUB@aol.com

VISA   **MasterCard**

PRICES SUBJECT TO CHANGE WITHOUT NOTICE

FOR MORE INFORMATION ON BOOKS OR SUPPLIES CALL OR WRITE US

WE ARE ALWAYS GLAD TO HEAR FROM YOU!

Susan Scheewe Publications Inc.

13435 N.E. Whitaker Way   Portland, Or. 97230   PH (503)254-9100   FAX (503)252-9508

WATERCOLOR BOOKS

Vol. 20	"Simply Country Watercolors" by Susan Scheewe Brown	257	$9.50 ___
Vol. 21	"Simply Watercolor" by Susan Scheewe Brown.....T.V. Book	260	$11.95 ___
Vol. 24	"Introduction to Watercolor" by Susan Scheewe Brown.....T.V. Book	314	$11.95 ___
Vol. 25	"Watercolors Anyone Can Paint" by Susan Scheewe Brown...T.V. Book	325	$11.95 ___
Vol. 26	"Watercolor - The Garden Scene" by Susan Scheewe Brown... T.V. Book	339	$11.95 ___
Vol. 27	"Watercolor Landscapes" by Susan Scheewe Brown....T.V. Book	360	$11.95 ___
Vol. 28	"Watercolor - Garden Treasures" by Susan Scheewe Brown....T.V. Book	361	$11.95 ___
Vol. 29	"Watercolor Collection" by Susan Scheewe Brown....T.V. Book	374	$11.95 ___
*NEW Vol. 30	"Scheewe Art Workshop - Watercolor & Acrylic" by Susan Scheewe Brown..T.V. Bk.	398	$11.95 ___
*NEW Vol. 31	"Enjoy Watercolor & Acrylic" by Susan Scheewe Brown.....T.V. Book	399	$11.95 ___
*NEW Vol. 32	"Le Jardin" by Susan Scheewe Brown.....T.V. Book	414	$12.95 ___
*NEW Vol. 33	"Simply Acrylic & Watercolor" by Susan Scheewe Brown.....T.V. Book	418	$12.95 ___
Vol. 7	"Watercolor Journey" by Ellie Cook	381	$9.50 ___
Vol. 3	"Watercolor Made Easy 3" by Kathy George	301	$9.50 ___
*NEW Vol. 1	"Watercolor for Real" by Robert and Sharon Long	409	$9.50 ___
Vol. 1	"The Way I Started" by Gary Hawk	120	$6.00 ___
Vol. 1	"Watercolor Fun & Easy" by Beverly Kaiser	243	$7.50 ___
Vol. 7	"Watercolor Charms" by Sharon Rachal	376	$9.50 ___

VIDEOS BY SUSAN SCHEEWE BROWN

"Scheewe Art Workshop I" 13-1/2 HR Shows On 4 Tapes/ Introduction to Watercolors	S8225	$69.99
"Scheewe Art Workshop II" 13-1/2 HR Shows On 4 Tapes/ Watercolors Anyone Can Paint...	S8223	$69.99
"Scheewe Art Workshop III" 13 - 1/2 HR Shows On 4 Tapes/ The Garden Scene	S8375	$69.99
"Scheewe Art Workshop III B" 13 - 1/2 HR Shows On 4 Tapes/ Watercolor Landscapes	S8376	$69.99
"Watercolor Painting with Children" 1 Hour	S8222	$19.99 ___
"Fabric Painting Fun" 1 Hour		$24.99 ___
"Watercolor Techniques" 1 Hour	S8226	$19.99 ___
"Painting Projects" Watercolor 3 Hours...Trees and Leaves	S8224	$49.99 ___
"Acrylic Techniques For Everyone" I Hour	S8368	$19.99 ___

PEN & INK BOOKS / COLORED PENCIL BOOKS

Vol. 6	"Journey of Memories" by Claudia Nice	166	$6.50 ___
Vol. 7	"Scenes from Seasons Past" by Claudia Nice	183	$9.50 ___
Vol. 8	"Taste of Summer" by Claudia Nice	223	$9.50 ___
Vol. 2	"Colored Pencil Made Easy" by Jane Wunder	242	$7.50 ___
Vol. 3	"The Beauty of Colored Pencil and Ink Drawing" by Jane Wunder	259	$7.50 ___
Vol. 4	"Watercolor, Pen and Ink" by Jane Wunder	357	$9.50 ___
Vol. 5	"Watercolor, Pen and Ink, Vol. 2" by Jane Wunder..........*NEW.	422	$9.50 ___

OILS BOOKS

Vol. 1	"His and Hers" by Susan Scheewe	101	$6.50 ___
Vol. 7	"Paint 'n Patch" by Susan Scheewe	107	$5.50 ___
Vol. 11	"I Love To Paint" by Susan Scheewe	111	$6.50 ___
Vol. 14	"Enjoy Painting Animals" by Susan Scheewe	114	$6.50 ___
Vol. 19	"Gift Of Painting" by Susan Scheewe O/AC/WC	230	$9.50 ___
Vol. 1	"Western Images" by Becky Anthony	186	$6.50 ___
Vol. 5	"Soft Petals" by Georgia Bartlett	171	$6.50 ___
Vol. 6	"Painting Fantasy Flowers" by Georgia Bartlett	215	$7.50 ___
Vol. 8	"Petals" by Georgia Bartlett	317	$9.50 ___
Vol. 9	"Floral Medley" by Georgia Bartlett	344	$9.50 ___
Vol. 10	"Flower Show" by Georgia Bartlett..........*NEW	415	$9.50 ___
Vol. 4	"Countryscapes" by Donna Bell	249	$9.50 ___
Vol. 5	"Painter to Painter" by Donna Bell	263	$9.50 ___
Vol. 6	"Landscapes With Acrylics & Oil" by Donna Bell	282	$9.50 ___
Vol. 1	"Natures Palette" by Carol Binford.....O/AC	248	$9.50 ___
Vol. 2	"Oil Painting The Easy Way" by Bill Blackman	337	$9.50 ___
Vol. 3	"Lighted Windows & Gardens" by Bill Blackman	355	$9.50 ___
Vol. 1	"Mini Mini More" by Terri and Nancy Brown	150	$6.50 ___
Vol. 2	"Mini Mini More" by Terri and Nancy Brown	151	$6.50 ___
Vol. 4	"Heritage Trails" by Terri and Nancy Brown	169	$6.50 ___
Vol. 7	"More Garden Trails" by Terri and Nancy Brown	368	$9.50 ___
Vol. 2	"Windows of My World" by Jackie Claflin	181	$9.50 ___
Vol. 4	"Windows Of My World 4" by Jackie Claflin	359	$9.50 ___
Vol. 4	"Expressions In Oil" by Delores Egger	239	$7.50 ___
Vol. 2	"Days of Heaven" by Gloria Gaffney	252	$9.50 ___
Vol .6	"The Sky's The Limit" by Jean Green	372	$9.50 ___
Vol. 3	"Nature's Beauty" by Bill Huffaker	177	$6.50 ___
Vol. 1	"Ducks and Geese" by Jean Lyles	172	$6.50 ___
Vol. 1	"Raining Cats & Dogs" by Todd Mallett	304	$9.50 ___
Vol. 2	"Another Path To Follow" by Lee McGowen	328	$9.50 ___
Vol. 1	"Bitterroot Backroads" by Glenice Moore-Nickel	330	$9.50 ___
Vol. 2	"Bitterroot Backroads 2" by Glenice Moore-Nickel	340	$9.50 ___
Vol. 3	"Bitterroot Backroads 3" by Glenice Moore-Nickel	369	$9.50 ___
Vol. 1	"Stepping Stones" by Judy Nutter	121	$6.50 ___
Vol. 1	"Painting with Paulson" by Buck Paulson	343	$11.95 ___
Vol. 1	"Rustic Charms" by Sharon Rachal	175	$6.50 ___
Vol. 2	"Rustic Charms II" by Sharon Rachal	199	$9.50 ___
Vol. 5	"Rustic Charms V, Florals" by Sharon Rachal	261	$9.50 ___
Vol. 1	"Painting Flowers With Augie" by Augie Reis	152	$6.50 ___
Vol. 3	"Realistic Technique" by Judy Sleight	341	$9.50 ___
Vol. 2	"Soft & Misty Paintings" by Kathy Snider	229	$9.50 ___
Vol. 4	"Friends We've Known" by Gene Waggoner	187	$7.50 ___
Vol. 5	"Friends Are Forever" by Gene Waggoner	231	$7.50 ___
Vol. 1	"Fantasy Folk" by Don Weed	123	$6.50 ___
Vol. 1	"Something Special For Everyone" by Mildred Yeiser	158	$6.50 ___
Vol. 5	"Soft & Gentle Paintings" by Mildred Yeiser	268	$9.50 ___

SHIPPING & HANDLING CHARGES
Add $3.00 for the First Book for shipping and handling.
Add $1.50 per each additional book.
Please Add $4.00 for handling & postage. PER TAPES. Sorry
we must have a "NO REFUND - NO RETURN" policy.
U.S CURRENCY